Penpal

PROGRAMS

In Primary Classrooms

DEBORAH P. BERRILL

MOLLY GALL

Pembroke Publishers Limited

Acknowledgements

We wish to acknowledge the contributions of the more than thirty participating classroom teachers and over sixty student teacher classroom coordinators who contributed their expertise to this penpal program. Their words and practices have informed the continual evolution of the program.

A special thanks to Lois Biddle, Sharon Maskell and Janice Mackenzie whose ideas and enthusiasm helped build the foundation of this penpal program and to Brenda Chatten and Kim Kasperski who initiated the program as student teachers.

And, of course, our admiration goes to the university students who provide genuine caring and strong motivation for emergent reader/writers; and to the children who find their own voices in these relationships through reading and writing.

© 2000 Pembroke Publishers
538 Hood Road
Markham, Ontario, Canada L3R 3K9
www.pembrokepublishers.com

Distributed in the U.S. by Stenhouse Publishers
477 Congress Street
Portland, ME 04101
www.stenhouse.com

We acknowledge the financial support of the Government of Canada through the Book Publishing Industry Development Program (BPIDP) for our publishing activities.

Canadian Cataloguing in Publication Data

Berrill, Deborah P
    Penpal programs in primary classrooms

Includes index.
ISBN 1-55138-124-9

1. English language – Composition and exercises – Study and teaching (Primary).
2. Letter writing – Study and teaching (Primary). 3. Pen pals – Study and teaching (Primary). I. Gall, Molly. II. Title.
LB1528.B47 2000   372.62'3044   C00-931562-4

Editor: Cynthia Young
Cover Design: John Zehethofer
Cover Photography: Ajay Photographics
Typesetting: JayTee Graphics

Printed and bound in Canada
9 8 7 6 5 4 3 2 1

Penpal Programs in Primary Classrooms

Table of Contents

Why a Penpal Program?

Introduction

Skill Development Through Friendship

This book has grown from our ten-year involvement in a penpal letter-writing program. We have learned many things that help us run our program more smoothly — and more efficiently. We found a need for certain structures to ensure the timely and continuous exchange of letters, ongoing support for the relationship between the writers, and wise use of classroom time. And though much of this book is devoted to those structures, we know that other teachers in other classrooms might do things differently for their own reasons. Please adapt our suggestions to suit your needs. Our real intention is to offer help, so that when more than twenty-five letters arrive, and more than twenty-five eager but not-yet-literate young students want to read those letters, classroom teachers will not feel overwhelmed.

In our program, the penpals are in the same city, and there are many benefits to this. Being in the same city enables us to find affordable ways to exchange letters. In addition, being in the same city gives the penpals the opportunity to physically meet each other very early in the program.

Although we have tried some e-mail letter exchange, our program is based on having children write their letters by hand rather than compose them on the computer. Handwritten letters allow the classroom teacher to observe several very important aspects of language development, such as letter formation, spacing of words, use of punctuation and capitalization — things that many computer software programs take care of automatically.

Volunteer assistants can be a valuable resource for some teachers in the program. Whether you use adult volunteers or other children who are more accomplished readers, volunteers provide one-on-one support for children who really need it.

Anyone who sees the children when they receive their penpal letters cannot help but note their excitement — certainly about receiving their very own letters — but also about writing back to their penpals. And it is this enthusiasm, even by struggling reader/writers, that demonstrates just how powerful a penpal relationship can be in helping children learn to read and write. This powerfulness comes from the relationship between the correspondents and the real and purposeful nature of the writing. Children are not writing for their teacher: They are writing to and for their penpals.

Even the most emergent reader/writers quickly learn to recognize their own names and take strong ownership over their letters. The children decide whether or not to have someone help them read the letter. Many take their letters home to share with their families. The children also decide what they will say in reply to their penpals, even though they may not be able to *scribe* the words by themselves.

In the penpal program, children are not chastised for not being able to "write," because they all *do* write, in one fashion or another. That, too, is part of the success. The children are welcomed as part of the reading/writing club from the very first letter they receive from their penpals. That first letter is an invitation to become friends, and we have never seen a child refuse the invitation.

This friendship is different because it begins with and is developed through written language. Not only are the children motivated to read and write, but they are also shown the power of language in human interaction. Children in this program discover that their words, no matter how halting, are received and valued; and that regardless of how developed or undeveloped their writing is, their written language is meaningful and prompts written responses that can be read over and over.

The children also know that their older penpals value their letters. Older penpals tell the children how glad they were to receive a letter, where they put up the children's drawings, and the names of friends who read the letter. Just visit the rooms of these older penpals to see how important the children's letters and pictures are. Indeed, they are on bulletin boards, on doors, and on walls next to beds!

Beyond Skill Development: Supporting Human Connection and Caring

As the letter writing continues through the year, the older penpal provides ongoing support to the younger penpal as a reader/writer. The program offers an opportunity for the development of a human relationship where the child is the center of positive attention from a person who plays a small but increasingly significant role in the child's life. The emotional attachment that is fostered is a very significant factor in the children's motivation to write. This attachment is expressed continually through words and symbols and is part of what we consider the mentoring that occurs in the program.

Letters from the older penpals provide scaffolding support for the younger reader/writers, who are encouraged to use the older penpals' letters in their responses. They learn to use their penpals' letters to become more independent in their own writing.

As classroom teachers become familiar with the penpal program, they see ways that this relationship-through-writing can be used to stretch each child, according to her or his own needs and abilities. This book will demonstrate the kinds of "incidental" teaching that can occur in one-on-one situations through the letter-writing and -reading — teaching that receives little attention, but which may well provide the most significant learning opportunities for many children.

When we review the program at the end of each year, we are reminded about how deeply each of us values the kinds of things that happen because of it. We see children who recognize the power of their own written words; children who know the satisfaction of communicating over time with another person who has demonstrated their interest in and caring for them; children who know that they can write and read, and that even if they can't do it as well as some others that they can still make their ideas known through writing.

Assumptions About Language Arts Teaching

The teachers involved in a penpal program have many different kinds of classrooms. That is one of the great strengths of the program: It can be implemented in a variety of language arts programs and by teachers who may have different philosophies of teaching. Despite their differences, teachers involved in the program do share some common assumptions about language arts teaching.

- *Good language teaching and learning has been going on for a very long time.*

Many aspects of traditional classrooms have provided wonderful environments for children to learn to write and read, and to associate reading and writing with pleasure and success. It is important not to abandon these practices just because they have been in use for a long time. Sometimes that is precisely why they should be kept.

However, teachers can make better use of classroom time when they understand different strategies and what makes them more effective or less effective. The issue then becomes how much time to devote to a particular strategy, rather than whether or not to incorportate that strategy.

- *There is no single "best" way to learn.*

Many people feel very strongly about how language teaching/learning should occur. Far too often, different approaches are placed in opposition, with proponents of this approach or that approach claiming full rights for only their method. Thus, teachers may be urged to use only a phonics approach (or basal readers, or experience charts, or whole language), and they come away with the understanding that any inclusion from "opposing" approaches is heresy.

However, we believe that different people learn in different ways — and even that the same person may learn in different ways at different times. Therefore, teachers must provide opportunities for different ways of learning how to read and write. There may be a place for isolated skill teaching, as well as language-rich environments where reading and writing are viewed as interconnected processes. We recognize and value independent writing and reading activities as much as we do interdependent, social activities. Research shows that many language activities are more social than first thought.

It is impossible to make every option available at all times. However, teachers can rely on their students to help them understand how they, as individual students, learn best at any given time. Teachers can then use that information to structure their classrooms to offer as many diverse learning opportunities as possible.

- *Classrooms should be print-rich.*

Most teachers find that a print-rich environment is essential in the approach to literacy in the penpal program. Print-rich classrooms help children become more independent. When children in a print-rich classroom ask how to spell a word, a suitable teacher repsonse is "Can you find that word somewhere in the room?" Children soon begin to use this strategy without prompting, and they can apply it successfully when they write their penpal letters.

- *Stretch each child and work with realistic language expectations for each child.*

Children, especially emergent reader/writers, need to feel success in their learning. It is important to start with each child's current abilities, then help them to stretch or develop their skills. As each child progresses, we can add appropriate challenges. In the penpal program, older penpals work one-on-one at the child's ability level. The older penpal provides challenge, taking the lead from the child's last letters.

- *Create opportunities for different kinds of writing.*

In most classrooms, children are encouraged to produce various kinds of writing: journal entries, stories, and books. The penpal

Print materials in the print-rich penpal classroom can be commercially produced or hand-printed/written items. Materials should come from a broad range of sources, including whole-class experience charts, chart stories, poems, words on graphs, library and text books, whole class and small group shared- reading activities, word lists (sight words and theme-related words and symbols), posters, magazines, news clippings — And of course, the letters to and from the penpals.

program adds letter writing and reading as real-world activities where children can apply and refine their skills.

A variety of reading and writing materials and genres is valued. A balanced variety of writing activities will encourage children to think in different ways and to communicate meaningfully. Penpal-letter writing is just one of many modes that can be used to create a balanced language arts program — but it is a particularly powerful one that is often absent in school.

- *Writing must be meaningful to the writer.*

Writing is one of the most powerful strategies for self-actualization. In order for writing to be powerful, it must be meaningful to its author. Learning to write is hard work for many children, so it is especially important that writing tasks be meaningful for emergent reader/writers. Calkins tells us that schools "set up roadblocks to stifle the natural and enduring reasons for writing." Sometimes the roadblocks are the result of artificial and de-contextualized writing assignments. When the purpose for writing is merely to complete an assignment, the writing is usually not very meaningful, especially for the writer. While it might allow a teacher to assess a child's achievement, such an assignment might not carry meaningfulness to the writer — especially if the achievement is low. The penpal program offers the advantage of inherent individual, affective, human connection that provides deep meaningfulness and purposefulness for most children.

- *Writing that emerges from a personal interest provides a meaningful context for writers.*

The penpal program provides a real context for children. Each child writes to a real person whom they meet (in our program), and with whom they develop a relationship over the year. Letters from the older penpals re-affirm the importance of the children's writing. Penpals ask and answer questions as they share personal information in their letters. The children know their questions are taken seriously: Their penpals answer them.

The penpal program helps children (and their penpals) recognize and experience the power of language in developing and maintaining human interconnectedness.

- *Knowledge is actively constructed through interaction with others and with the world.*

Students seem to learn best when they are active decision-makers. In the penpal program, the children choose what they want to write about. However, the teacher reminds children to answer their penpals' questions and helps them to recall activities that might be of interest to their penpals. This talk between teacher and child is not just "sharing"; it is a central part of the teaching/learning process. Brainstorming, topic selection, and word and sentence formation are enacted jointly by the child and the teacher. As the children become more proficient writers, these processes are internalized, and the children enact them independently. Penpals actively construct knowledge as they exchange letters. When penpals ask questions and share personal knowledge and expertise, they are constructing knowledge together. Research shows that we often learn of our own expertise and knowledge through our writing. In this way, the younger and older penpals both construct not only their knowledge, but their consciousness of that knowledge.

• *Writing and reading are complementary, interconnected processes.*

The interconnectedness of reading and writing that exists in many language situations is heightened in the penpal program. Many emergent readers in the program gain reading fluency through their writing. They learn conventions of spelling and punctuation and expand their vocabulary through writing and reading. Reading activities often result in a writing or thinking activity. Any story or information that is read is a potential prompt for a writing or talking/listening activity. Likewise, a writing activity can be a prompt for reading and talking/listening activities.

The penpal letters are prompts and resources for both reading and writing. When letters from the older penpals arrive, they are shared, usually with the whole class at "carpet" time. Children often re-read the letters, just for enjoyment, returning to earlier letters when they have become more proficient readers.

• *More experienced writers can be powerful mentors for emergent writers.*

Vyzgotsky 's term, the "Zone of Proximal Development," describes the difference between what learners can demonstrate on their own and what they can accomplish with assistance. Many teachers operate intuitively and frequently in their children's zones of proximal development, asking probing questions, prompting deeper reflection, encouraging independence.

The penpal program provides many opportunities for children to operate in their zones of proximal development. The penpal letters themselves become a presence of the children's mentors, asking questions while providing scaffolding for the child's response. In the ongoing penpal relationship, the risks that the children take are supported by models or resources that they learn to use by themselves.

How the Penpal Program Fits Into Wider Learning

We are not under the illusion that the penpal program is the only way a teacher should run a language arts program. We deeply value literature, poetry, story-writing, shared experience chart writing, chants, choral speaking, and all sorts of other language activities.

However, we know that the penpal program provides a different kind of motivation and experience. It allows children to reflect on their lives both in and out of school — and to receive feedback on that reflection. The penpal program also encourages non-narrative writing for a specific and tangible audience, thereby promoting thinking skills that other activities do not. Opportunities for this kind of thinking and writing can be hard to find. Penpal writing can enable children to go beyond the boundaries of the school in their learning process. The variety of letters that come into the classroom gives validity to many different ways of living and thinking. When we can match penpals by race, culture, and gender, many of our young writers connect with someone who also becomes a role model for them: someone who has experienced similar social or cultural activities; someone who has received similar responses to who they are as persons; someone who may have an unarticulated but deep understanding of the kinds of barriers a child is experiencing; and someone who has been successful in school and is pursuing post-secondary education.

Some children benefit most from the caring they receive from their penpal. The older penpal offers undivided attention and unconditional acceptance of the child, which conveys to the child a sense of worth and value. It is hard to quantify the importance of this aspect of the program, but it seems to be especially true if a child's home situation includes significant tension, if the family is struggling financially, or if the family is part of a marginalized group in the community. Consequently, the penpal program can provide a mentorship that extends well beyond language development.

Why Is Letter Writing Different From Other Writing?

Several different kinds of writing are found in early primary classrooms, such as charts and stories. And these kinds of writing are important. Narrative writing helps children make sense of and re-construct their lives in a very special way. It provides opportunities for children to recount or transform their life experiences within the community, to re-enact and test the validity of the norms in their community, and to consider ethical questions. Children discover certain kinds of patterns and connections in particular forms of writing. They begin to understand chronological sequence.

Yet, story reading and writing are different from letter reading and writing. The penpal program presents the opportunity to read and write in ways that other types of reading and writing usually do not allow. Letters have a general format that the children are encouraged to use. They are also instructed to ask questions (and to answer questions asked of them) in their letters. Unlike other forms of writing, penpal letter writing is a dialogue by its very nature. The exchange is meaningful and mutual. The penpals decide what they will share about themselves. They arrange the information and ideas differently than they would in stories. In part, this arrangement occurs because of the structures for organization and construction that develop over time between two people.

Increasingly, educational jurisdictions in English-speaking countries are adopting an expectations/outcomes-based approach to education, and teachers must provide opportunities for children to achieve those expectations. Most language arts curriculum expectations include the ability to use language confidently and competently in a variety of situations for communication, for personal satisfaction, and for learning; to enable [children] to participate fully in society; to organize information and ideas; to apply language conventions; to respond personally to text; and to participate in literacy communities.

The thinking and decision-making skills used in the penpal relationship differ from those in most other writing/reading activities. The closest thinking and decision-making situation may be sharing time, when the children can share something from their own lives with the class. However, there are things that many of us would not share in such a public forum that we might well share in the private penpal forum. These may pertain to a wide range of topics or issues, including exploration of things about ourselves. Such opportunity presents itself more easily through ongoing letter writing over time to an older and trusted individual. The extent to which this happens depends on a variety of things. In a safe atmosphere and social context, with an interested audience, the two penpals can communicate their ideas and personal responses meaningfully.

Emergent writers — whether they are children with special needs, are learning English as a second language, or are mainstream learners — benefit from penpal writing. Our penpal program follows the principles of the writing process. Moreover, penpal writing focuses on the "whole" language event, not just isolated sub-skills. Penpal writing takes into account the community and the socially interactive aspects of learning. Children use the letter writing genre experientially in their development of the language and communication skills that are at the heart of language arts expectations/standards. This kind of opportunity can be hard to find.

All these factors, along with the motivation that comes from the one-on-one relationship with an older penpal, are a significant part of what make this penpal program so powerful and successful for primary children.

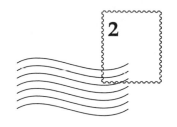

Setting Up a Penpal Program

Starting Out

Our penpal program has grown over the past ten years from two primary classrooms in a single school to eight primary classrooms in four elementary schools across the city. Originally, each child corresponded with a university student from a teacher education program. The penpal program was so popular, it was expanded to include other university students as well.

Our program grew quite large. However, certain organizational aspects will be much simpler for a single classroom teacher who is not involved in a wider program.

Larger Principles that Guide Our Annual Time Line

There are some larger principles that guide the development of our annual time line.

- Put the penpal program structures in place early. The penpal program will function best if both you and the coordinator of the older penpals have put the program structures in place by the end of August.
- The sooner in the school year the penpal program gets started, the better for everyone.
- Regardless of holidays or school/work pressures, it is important that letters be written and received on a regular basis.
- Large or small, penpal programs benefit from incorporating Penpal Days. Penpal Days provide opportunities for the penpal pairs to meet and get to know one another in person. This makes the letters easier to write because each penpal has met the "real"

person. This is especially important for younger writers because it gives them a tangible connection to their older penpal.

- Establishing letter deadlines and having penpals meet them is critical. Establish letter due dates with care. Double-check your calendar for any other events and responsibilities that could create a conflict for you, the coordinator, or the older penpals. For instance, most teachers would not want penpal letter writing just before report cards are due. Similarly, when setting the due dates for older penpals, consider their stress periods or holiday time. With university penpals, we ensured that no letters were due just before or during examinations. As well, university breaks do not always coincide with school breaks. Just remember, all of this is very manageable — It just takes a little foresight.

The Penpal Program, Language Arts, and Curriculum Expectations

We have found that many teachers are excited about the idea of a penpal program, but sometimes they do not stop to think fully about the ramifications of adding a penpal program to their existing program. Often, when new programs are thrust into a curriculum, the unexpected time involved to make the program run successfully is a source of stress and resentment.

There are many things to be considered in order to make time for this program. It is almost certain that some of your current activities and practices will have to be modified. It is impossible to anticipate *all* of the issues before the program begins; but, some pre-planning will help you recognize where things might need to be adapted and how much time must be allocated for penpal activities.

It is equally important to look at the language arts expectations, standards or outcomes required by your district's school board and to identify those which the penpal program will help achieve. If you know those expectations/standards, you will be able to meet them more readily through the penpal program. For instance, if your children are studying poetry, their letter that month could include a favorite poem. In the body of their letter, they might ask the penpal to write a poem or include their favorite poem in their reply. (We have found that poetry is often included serendipitously in February — around Valentine's Day. The "Roses are red..." variations are quite wonderful!)

There are several broad expectations that the penpal program can help you and your students meet in your own curriculum. These are listed in the table "Broad Expectations that Can Be Met through the Penpal Program" on page 15.

You can find additional ideas about the role that the penpal program can play in a language arts curriculum in Chapter 6: Assessing Language Arts Using Penpal Letters. You may want to scan that chapter for assistance during the set-up stage of your program.

Broad Expectations that Can Be Met through the Penpal Program

(These encompassing expectations have been modified from the National Council of Teachers of English, Standards for the English Language Arts (1997) and from the Western Canadian Protocol for Collaboration in Basic Education (1996), the Ontario Curriculum: English Language Arts (1999), The United Kingdom National Curriculum, 2000: Key Stage I (2000).)

- Respond to a wide range of print texts to build an understanding of texts, of themselves, and of the cultures of the diverse people around them, to acquire new information and for personal fulfillment.
- Read and write to explore thoughts, ideas, feelings, and experiences.
- Apply a wide range of strategies to comprehend, interpret, evaluate, and appreciate texts. Students draw on their prior experience, their interactions with other readers and writers, their knowledge of word meaning and of other texts, their word identification strategies, and their understanding of textual features (e.g., sound-letter correspondence, sentence structure, context, graphics).
- Adjust their use of spoken, written, and visual language (e.g., conventions, style, vocabulary) to communicate effectively with a variety of audiences and for different purposes.
- Employ a wide range of strategies as they write and use different writing process elements appropriately to communicate with different audiences for a variety of purposes.
- Apply knowledge of language structure, language conventions (e.g., spelling and punctuation), media techniques, figurative language, and genre to create, critique, and discuss print and nonprint texts.
- Develop an understanding of and respect for diversity in language use, patterns, and dialects across cultures, ethnic groups, geographic regions, and social roles.
- Participate as knowledgeable, reflective, creative, and critical members of a variety of literacy communities.
- Use spoken, written, and visual language to accomplish their own purposes (e.g., for learning, enjoyment, persuasion, and the exchange of information).
- Read and write to celebrate and build community.

How Much Time Does the Penpal Program Require?

Chances are your class will be made up of emergent writers, and there will be a wide range of reading/writing abilities. This program could be a huge time-consuming task. However, we have refined the process in order to accommodate various students' needs without consuming excessive blocks of time.

The time frame we use illustrates why it is important to think about how the penpal program will be integrated into your language arts program rather than being merely an "add on" to what already exists. Our way of running the penpal program requires approximately forty-five minutes a day of class time for

Approximate Time Frame for One Letter Reading and Writing Cycle	
Activity	Time per Cycle
Reading and sharing letters as a whole class	2 hours
Responding to letters	1–3 hours
Drawing pictures and making envelopes	1 hour

letter reading and writing, over approximately seven days each month. We share letters so that the children hear and see all of the letters, and this takes approximately two hours. Responding to letters takes one to three hours. Drawing pictures to include with letters, and decorating the envelopes, takes another hour. These drawing and decorating activities are very useful. Children who do not require assistance can continue to work on these two penpal-related activities, and the teacher has time to provide assistance to individual writers who need it. This helps tremendously in keeping the process manageable.

So, You Want to Start a Penpal Program?

So, you want to start a penpal program in your classroom? There are so many considerations, you might wonder just where to begin. Things can and should be done in increments. The following tips break up the tasks in ways that have worked well for us. You will probably find yourself doing a number of these things simultaneously, well before school start up in September. We find that using the Tips for Starting Up a Penpal Program are very helpful.

Finding Potential Older Writers

Initially this may appear to be your biggest challenge. It can be a daunting task just to figure out who to call in order to get started. Begin the search well before beginning the penpal program; that is, well before the school year begins. That way, the details can be sorted out while you are planning appropriate program integration with your language arts curriculum.

• *Local College or University*

If there is a local university with a teacher education program, call the teacher education (faculty of education) information telephone number and ask for the person in charge of Language Arts, Primary Education, or Elementary Education. (Different faculties of education organize themselves differently — but one of these areas should get you to the right person.) If one individual is not in charge, ask for the name of persons who teach Language Arts classes. Those people will be the most likely contact persons. If none of them is able to be the contact person, they will be able to suggest others who may be interested.

If the university does not have a teacher education program, contact either the Writing Program, a Child Studies Program, the Psychology Department, or the English Department. Early Childhood Education or Recreational Leadership programs in community colleges are also good sources for older penpals.

Follow the same procedures noted above if you contact different departments/institutions.

• *Local High School*

Contact the local area high school (the one most likely that the children in the school will eventually attend), and ask for the name of the Head of the English Department. If no one in the English Department is interested in participating, try the Family Studies Department, because Family Studies courses often include modules on child development.

• *Girl Scouts, Boy Scouts, 4-H Clubs and other Youth Groups/Organizations*

"Adopting" a whole class through letter writing may be a new idea for coordinators of these organizations, but the activity and involvement fits in with the philosophies of many of them. Check with the local Chamber of Commerce, your Volunteer Bureau, or organizations such as the YMCA to find out what organizations exist in your school's community.

Some very powerful connections can also be made through organizations that are working with adolescents who may be at risk themselves. Do not dismiss these young people, for as long as there is a responsible coordinator, there should be no risk for the children. And, the older penpals may be as changed by the experience as the young children; it may be the first responsibility of this sort that these adolescents have been given.

• *Senior Citizens' Organizations*

Almost every community has an umbrella group that organizes services and programs for seniors. Check with the Chamber of Commerce for a contact person. Then, explore the idea, being very explicit about the responsibilities of those involved in this program. (Seniors vary in their energy levels and their abilities to make the kind of commitment needed for this program.) Be sure to tell the contact person that this is a mentoring program, where the seniors become writer-mentors for the children. It is important that the seniors chosen will be able to write regularly and consistently, and that their penmanship is very readable or their letters can be word processed (either by them or by a volunteer).

Again, this type of matching can be much more beneficial than originally imagined, for many of our seniors are very active people with wonderful experiences to share. They often have little contact with very young children, and this sort of limited contact is ideal, for it allows a relationship to develop without over-taxing energy levels. As well, teachers might find that in addition to the writing connection, the senior penpals might come to school later in the year and share a skill with the children.

• *Business/Industry*

Our businesses and industries are often excellent school resources in unexpected ways. If persons from a local business/industry are enlisted as penpals, it is preferable to have all of the penpals from the same industry — it will greatly ease letter exchange. Just as for other groups noted above, it is important to have one-to-one penpal relationships. It is sometimes surprising just how receptive industry is to this kind of project and commitment. Our community businesses are often eager to be involved in meaningful ways with our schools — and sometimes neither they nor we know how to do that very well. This program provides an excellent opportunity for that kind of involvement. Remember as well, that the letters will be sent to the workplace or to the school, not to the penpals' homes. This ensures privacy for all penpals.

Teachers interested in pursuing the business/industry option can contact the Chamber of Commerce or the local Rotary Club. Both organizations will have helpful suggestions about businesses and industries that might participate, including the names of either the president or the staff relations/personnel director.

Tips for Starting Up a Penpal Program

Once you have decided to implement your own penpal program:

1. Locate a source of potential older penpals.

2. Discuss the program with your principal.

3. Find a population of older writers and a responsible person who is willing to coordinate them.

4. Set up a meeting with the coordinator of the older penpals to
   (a) establish guidelines and deadlines
   (b) match penpals, and
   (c) set up mailing or pick-up/drop off procedures for letter exchange.

5. Set up a meeting with the older penpals to inform them of your program and expectations. (This includes how you will run your program, what you are looking for from older penpals, the kind of writing, how to mentor, and so on.)
   Older penpals should be matched by the time this meeting occurs. You can inform them of who their younger penpal is at this meeting, as well as relaying the other pertinent information.

6. Inform your students' parents about the penpal program.

7. Recruit classroom volunteers or school buddies if they are needed for assistance in reading and writing letters.

8. With the coordinator, set up a Meet-Your-Penpal Day early in the writing relationship — preferably just after the first letter has been received from the older penpals.

Talking With the Principal

Before beginning a penpal program, teachers should discuss the program with their principal. This is especially important because the children will be involved in a relationship with young adults, who are initially strangers.

However, even before talking with the principal, get a clear picture in your own mind of just what will happen in the program. The Tips For Starting Up a Penpal Program provides a convenient checklist of things that need to be done.

Some principals may be concerned about costs. Though there are not many, there are some expenses associated with the way we run the program. These include photocopying costs (of penpal letters) and travel costs on the "Penpal Days," where older and younger penpals meet face to face.

Principals will require an overview of the program. They will want a general understanding of how this program fits into the language arts program and the kinds of language expectations the penpal program will help achieve. The general Penpal Program Overview provides an initial introduction to the program and can be shown to the principal. Reassure the principal about how parents will be informed about this program. A copy of the Penpal Program Overview along with the statement explaining how the penpal program fits into the Language Arts and how it can help to meet individual needs can be sent with the letter to the parents.

The principal may also have some administrative rules you must follow. For instance, some school boards might ask that each of the older penpals get a Criminal Offenses Screening or similar police clearance. A copy of this can be forwarded to the principal to be kept on file.

Finding a Coordinator

Another key to a successful penpal program is having good help. Once you have located a group of people willing to be penpals, you will need to identify a coordinator for those writers. The coordinator coordinates the older penpals for a single classroom. (That means that if you are doing this in a multiple-classroom setting, it is wise to have one coordinator for each classroom.) The coordinator will need time to get organizational details in place, too. Therefore, it is a good idea to enlist your coordinator as soon as possible once you have decided to run a penpal program.

Inform the coordinator that they will be responsible for ensuring that older penpals meet their commitments. Sometimes the coordination takes very little time; but, if there are any problems with delinquent writers, the amount of time needed increases considerably. The coordinator must maintain regular contact with the classroom teacher to stay abreast of delinquent writers, or of other issues which may arise.

Penpal Program Overview

The Penpal Program is classroom-based. That is, whole classrooms are involved, not individual students in different classes, or only some students in a given class. The letters are sent to the school, not to any penpal's home. Teachers integrate letter-writing and reading into their Language Arts programs and are able to monitor the writing development of the children very closely through keeping Penpal Folders. Parents are very interested in seeing the progress of their children as demonstrated by the letters they have written over the school year.

The program matches students from the university program with students in primary classrooms: and penpals write letters to each other every three to four weeks for most of the school year. These letter-writing activities are part of the classroom Language Arts program. After the letters are photocopied, the children take them home to share with their families.

A "Meet-Your-Penpal" day is held in early autumn, and all of the children come to the university to meet their penpals. Children and their penpals either complete an identification of buildings "treasure hunt," or they participate in various other activities, ranging from running obstacle courses to doing leaf drawings. Refreshments are served, and by the end of an hour and a half, the penpals have had a chance to talk with each other and to get to know each other much more quickly than they would through letters alone. (This is especially true for the children.) Parents/guardians are welcome to attend as well: They have a chance to meet the person who will be writing to their child and to talk with the coordinator of the program, the classroom coordinators, and the classroom teacher.

Midway through the year, the children host their penpals at their school. Children send invitations, decide how to entertain their penpals, and make refreshments. The older penpals get a chance to see the children in their school setting.

The letter writing ceases towards the end of the university year — usually in late March/early April. During the year, the children will have written between six and eight letters to their older penpals. They will have established a connection with a young adult who has acted as a friend and mentor for them, helping them improve their reading and writing through friendship.

How Our Penpal Program Fits Into Our Language Arts Program

The letters that the children write to their penpal are only part of our writing and reading program. Our whole program consists of many activities in addition to the emphasis that we put on penpal letters; things such as language awareness, including attention to letter sounds, phonics, and the meaning of conventions of written communication.

Some of these activities include writing workshops, writing whole-class experience charts, story writing and individual reading of books. If you have questions about the direct teaching of language skills, please ask me. I will be pleased to explain how we do these things.

Therefore, the letter writing and reading that we do provides an opportunity for the children to demonstrate what they can actually do, as well as to learn to do new things with the guidance of their older penpal's letter and the classroom teacher.

As in all of our Language Arts programming, our objective is to help the children become as independent as possible in their writing and their reading.

Date:_____

Dear Parent/Guardian,

In conjunction with [source of older penpals: _____], our class is involved in a penpal exchange. Each child in the class is matched with a [_____] and these pairs of students become Penpals for the school year, writing each other through their respective school addresses.

   Our Penpal Program is classroom-based, which means that the whole classroom is involved, not just individual students. We integrate letter-writing and reading into our Language Arts program and I am able to monitor the writing development of the children very closely.

   The children feel special and proud of themselves because of their relationship with [source of older penpals: _____] who provide the incentive and motivation to write. We see much development in the children's letters over the course of the year and are delighted to be able to be part of this Penpal Program. Ask your child to share their penpal letters with you each month. You'll be pleased at the progress you see in your child's reading and writing.

   If you have any questions, don't hesitate to contact me at the school.

Sincerely,

Classroom teacher

Oftentimes, the coordinator ends up being the teacher's initial contact person from that group — the person with whom the teacher has negotiated all along. However, it is not necessary that the initial contact person fill that role.

We have found that a responsible person from the group (even from a student group) can fulfill the expectations very well. The essential thing is that this person understands the nature and seriousness of the role of coordinator before taking it on. As well, if your older penpals and coordinator are high school students, the coordinator will need the strong support of a teacher advisor who can help deal with problem issues if they arise.

Although it was not possible when we first started up our program, we now require that a coordinator has been a penpal first. This way, the person understands the details of letter writing; the anticipation in waiting for their letter to arrive; the great pleasure that comes in meeting their penpal; and, ultimately, the importance of each individual writer.

The Matching Meeting

The Matching Meeting typically occurs as quickly as possible in September — once the coordinator has your class list. This meeting provides an opportunity for you to meet the penpals; to tell them about the children, both globally and individually; and to explain how the penpal program fits into the Language Arts program. You can also assess the appropriateness of all the penpal matches and make any changes that will enhance the penpal relationships, such as closer ethnic or heritage matching. The coordinator should provide the older penpals with more details about the organization and expectations of the penpal program. At the end of this meeting, the older penpals receive the name of their individual penpal.

The coordinator should prepare support materials to distribute to the older penpals. These materials are discussed in Chapter 3 and include a welcoming letter from the coordinator, a writing schedule, a model envelope, technical tips for writing, content suggestions, and common grammatical errors to avoid.

As the classroom teacher, you need to talk to the group about your class as a whole, as well as your Language Arts program and how the penpal program fits into it. We have found that samples of letters from both the older penpals and the children are quite helpful at this meeting. Many older penpals find that receiving an outline of expectations and suggestions specific to the class is very useful.

Having the *classroom teacher* share this information helps immensely in several ways. It emphasizes just how important their letters are to the children. The older penpals get an idea of "the big picture," enabling them to see how their letters fit into the wider curriculum. They see concrete examples of writing that

If possible, hold this meeting in the early evening, so that appropriate school personnel and the university students can attend. It takes approximately one hour to explain the necessary information to the older penpals.

children have done. Many non-teachers do not know a lot about early writing skills. The samples demonstrate skill levels typical of young children. Seeing the examples helps the older penpals get a feel for an appropriate level of writing and length of letter for their child.

We have also found it to be very beneficial to bring photographs of the children to this meeting. The photograph — a face to match to the name — helps the older penpals write more personally. And on Penpal Day, they can find their younger friend more quickly.

The Matching Meeting: Tips for Teachers

There are several major reasons that teachers are part of the Matching Meeting.

1. To meet the older penpals so that
   (a) matching changes can be made if it seems desirable for closer matching, and
   (b) any follow up is easier.

2. To introduce the older penpals to the kinds of things that happen in the teacher's Language Arts program, so that they understand the importance of their writing in the children's language learning.

3. To teach the older penpals about who six-year-olds are: their worlds; their emerging abilities; and their need for support.

4. To show the older penpals examples of the children's work so that the older penpals can target their letters to an appropriate level.

5. If possible, to give the older penpals photographs of the children.

6. To reinforce the importance of the older penpals in the lives of these children.

Things teachers will want to bring with them:

- samples of children's work
- photographs of the children
- a letter to the penpals from the teacher welcoming them, and indicating topics presently being studied in the classroom. This letter can be printed or word processed with appropriate size print (or computer font) for children of this age.

• Older Penpals and the Nature of Emergent Writing

It is crucial for older penpals to understand the nature of emergent writing. This can become a much larger issue than anticipated. Older penpals need to have appropriate expectations for the children's letters before the program starts. Do a short presentation about how writing develops to help older penpals avoid misunderstandings. This presentation is an ideal time to distribute "The Early Development of Writing" handout.

Ensure that older penpals understand the nature of spelling development and your expectations of the children regarding spelling. Explain how you teach spelling and what to watch for in the progression of spelling development (that is, if the older penpals are going to receive copies of the draft letters as well as the final copies).

It is very important that the older penpals use conventional spelling and that their letters be as error-free as possible. Explain that the children use their letters as models of conventional writing and spelling. Also advise the older penpals of how you intend to "use" their letters as part of your teaching (e.g., Word Detective, in which the children might circle all the words in the letter they can read on their own).

Penpal Days

The other important days that involve the classroom teachers are the Penpal Days. On Penpal Days, the older and younger penpals get together, physically. The first of these occurs in the early autumn, as soon as the children complete their first letter in response to their older penpals' initial letters. This is hosted by the older penpals at their site, and they arrange for the activities of the event. However, it is your responsibility to get the children to this event (probably a bus will be needed), and to find additional chaperones to help you on the trip.

Although the children will receive their first letter by "mail" (or no-cost school board courier, or a pick-up location), they take their first reply (letter and drawing) to the Meet-Your-Penpal Day, rather than "mailing" it. This saves time in getting the letter exchange fully implemented, produces an activity for Meet-Your-Penpal Day that is focused directly on the children and on reading/writing, and provides a way for the older penpals to discover more about the reading/writing development of their younger penpal.

The second Penpal Day is held in mid-way through the writing year, when the older penpals visit the children at the school. As the classroom teacher, you are responsible for organizing this day, with help from volunteers, and including ideas from the children.

Some time during the Meet-Your-Penpal Day must be set aside so the children can read their letters to their penpals and talk about their drawings.

This sharing is very motivating for the children: They experience the enthusiasm of their older penpals. As well, however, this sharing emphasizes to the older penpals, as nothing else can, just how dependent their emergent writer may be, and this seems to help the older writers take more care in their letters and be more helpful mentors.

Date:_____

Dear Penpal,

The student with whom you will be exchanging letters is in grade two. Our students are aged six or seven, and a couple of them are eight. Our students range from very beginning readers to a little more experienced readers. The beginning readers are basically reading consonant–vowel–consonant words (i.e., bug, hat).

Please keep your letters short and simple at this time of the year and limit the number of questions you ask to two or three. If you are writing your letter by hand, please make sure that your letters are printed, using the correct upper and lower case letters. The letters should also be large and legible. If you are using a computer, please use a font that makes an "a" like this "a."

Small drawings to illustrate more challenging words are helpful. The children love lots of color in their letters and get excited over envelopes or letters that have interesting decorations. They also enjoy getting a photograph of their penpal as well as an enclosure of pictures or drawings.

If you are looking for suggestions for your letter, we are currently learning about _____. We have a rabbit and a frog in our classroom, and our class does all the composting for the school.

If you have any questions, please contact me at school (telephone number:_____) or e-mail me at the school (e-mail address:_____). The children are very excited that they will be getting their "very own" penpal! I hope that this will be both a fun and educational experience for you!

Yours,

_____

Classroom teacher

The Early Development of Writing: What to Look for in Penpal Letters

With emergent writers, there are several things that you can watch for which will help you recognize a child's writing development. We expect a vast range of development with young children. Oftentimes it is very helpful to understand the logic of writing which may initially appear illogical or random to those unfamiliar with how writing develops. It will be most satisfying to you if you can identify specific things in the writing which demonstrate what your penpal can do, rather than just focusing on the things that are not yet mastered.

It is also very helpful to the child if you celebrate her/his accomplishments by noting (in your letter to the child) something the child has demonstrated in her/his letter to you which was not evident in previous letters.

Early Emergent Writing

1. Scribbles to express ideas.

2. Can distinguish between drawing and writing.

3. Uses own symbols to write (even if these are not conventional letter symbols).

4. Writes from left to right and from the top to the bottom of the page.

5. Uses letters or letter-like shapes.

6. Understands letter/sound relationships.

7. Writes clusters or combinations of letters; is prepared to invent spelling for words.

8. Can use spaced clusters of letters to create sentences.

9. Writes single known words.

10. Writes simple sentences using approximated spelling.

(from McGregor & Meiers, (1987) Writing K - 12: A Guide to Assessment & Reporting. Victoria, Australia: The English Club.)

Annual Timeline For the Penpal Program

Month	Week	What should happen
August		– coordinator(s) and classroom teacher(s) meet to discuss the penpal program details
		– set the dates for the Matching Meeting, Penpal Days, and penpal letter deadlines for the whole year for both the older penpals and the children
September	1	– older penpals sign up for the program; this can be done earlier if the program uses penpals that are not high school or university students
		– classroom teacher(s) compiles and delivers class list to coordinator(s) by the end of this week
	2	– coordinator(s) matches penpals
	3	– Matching Meeting, with all older penpals, classroom coordinators, classroom teachers
	4	– older penpals write the first letter, introducing themselves and inviting the children to Meet-Your-Penpal Day
		– coordinator(s) and volunteer older penpals plan Meet-Your-Penpal Day
October	1	– children receive the first letter by the end of the first week and begin composing their first letters back
	2	– older penpals host Meet-Your-Penpal Day
		– children bring their first letter with them and read it to or with their penpal and talk about their drawing
	3	– older penpals write their second letter to the children
November – March		– letter writing/exchange continues, with letters being exchanged approximately every two weeks; each correspondent writes approximately one letter/month
January		– children include invitations for the School Penpal Day in their letters to older penpals
		– the classroom coordinator is also invited
February		– children host the School Penpal Day
		– older penpals bring a letter and have their penpal read it to them
March/ April		– end of the university academic term approaches
		– several weeks prior to the end of their academic year, older penpals write their "last letter" to their penpal, explaining that it is the "last letter"
		(**Note:** It is important to end the writing by May.)
May/June		– debriefing session: coordinator(s) and classroom teacher(s) discuss the program and determine things to keep; things to change; things to eliminate

Using the Penpal Letters for Learning and Assessment

As we will demonstrate in Chapter 8: Assessing Language Arts Using Penpal Letters, the letters themselves should become part of the battery of assessment tasks used in the Language Arts program. Knowing this may make it easier to decide how to modify your existing language arts programming to accommodate the letter reading and writing.

After the child has read their letter from their older penpal, if possible, we highly recommend that the letter be photocopied. The original can go home and the photocopy is kept in the child's folder for later use in reading and writing activities. One of the first things that a child can do is to circle all of the words that they can read independently. This is especially helpful with emergent and early writers, giving a dated demonstration of word recognition skills, which you may wish to incorporate into your reading grade for the child. If this reading activity is included, there might be other reading activities that can be eliminated, compacted, or combined.

Making photocopies of the older penpals' letters is a personal choice for each individual teacher. A photocopy has many uses in that the children can circle questions or question marks and write directly on the letter for ideas about responding. It can be used to track the overall communication between the penpals.

However, photocopying is time consuming and most teachers have a volunteer do this task. As well, depending on school budgets, it may not be a feasible expenditure. However, because of the great advantages to having copies of letters, we do encourage you to explore this option as much as possible.

Essentials Needed to Establish Regular Communication

In planning a penpal program, there are a number of essentials to bear in mind. We have learned that in order for the program to run smoothly and to achieve our primary purpose, it is crucial that letters are exchanged on a regular basis. Although this seems self-evident and straightforward, it can become problematic if either the child or the older penpal is delinquent in their letter writing. Some of our structures have been developed specifically to ensure that regular communication occurs.

• *There must be a contact person who coordinates the older penpals: the coordinator.*

We have always operated on the assumption that this is a classroom-based program: that is, every child in a classroom has a penpal and letters are sent to the school (or workplace)—not to anyone's home. When new children join the class, someone needs to find a penpal for them. It is not easy for classroom teachers to find additional penpals by themselves, so we have found having a contact person (coordinator) for the older penpals is essential. The coordinator works closely with the classroom teacher and has multiple responsibilities. With the classroom teacher, they establish due dates for letters, both for older penpals and for children; the Matching Meeting; and the first Penpal Day. They also arrange transportation to the school for the second Penpal Day; they find additional penpals when new children join the classroom; and, they debrief the program with the classroom teacher at the end of the year.

- *There must be a no-cost or very low-cost way for "mailing" the letters, such as a school board courier system, or a person who physically carries the letters to and from the school.*

We have used a school board courier system or a contact person and drop-off location to exchange our letters. Depending on the size of the community in which you live, a drop-off location might be the school itself, the home of the coordinator or the classroom teacher, or a common time and meeting spot for handing over the letters. What is essential is that transportation of the letters does not involve cost. Postage can easily become an issue for either the older penpals or the younger ones.

Using a courier system of some sort , in which all letters are sent in a bunch, has other advantages. With a courier system, everyone understands that their letters must be ready for a given day, and this type of deadline is helpful for all writers. The program is much more manageable when all the letters arrive together and when all of the children's letters are sent out together. It does not take very long for writers to remember they must have a completed letter ready every other Tuesday (for instance). This helps writers of all ages to be thinking subconsciously about what they might write and what joke, riddle, puzzle, or drawing they might include in their letter. Writing process research indicates just how valuable this kind of pre-planning is for successful writing.

- *Classroom volunteers or school buddies may be needed for assistance in reading and writing letters.*

A volunteer may be needed to help in the classroom — especially for writing the first letter. There are pros and cons to this, for it is important that the children compose their own letters. Volunteers who are not trained may not realize the extent to which they may be taking the children's voice from them. Some teachers prefer to have volunteers just for the first letter so that they have a bit more control over a potentially chaotic situation. If teachers do not have access to adult volunteers or school buddies, and depending on the reading abilities of the children, they will want to explore other possibilities at their school. (See Chapter 4 for specifics for volunteers, including handouts you can give them.)

- *With young writers, it is essential that the penpals have an opportunity to meet each other early in the writing relationship — preferably after just one letter has been received from the older penpals.*

This first Penpal Day provides an opportunity for the penpals to get to know each other as real people. This makes a profound difference in establishing a relationship — both for younger and older penpals. It is important that activities are planned ahead for this meeting. Like any people meeting for the first time, planned activities will help the penpals get to know each other much more easily.

• Easy access to a photocopier helps you make maximum curricular use of the letters.

We strongly recommend that original drafts of children's letters be kept or photocopied so that you have a record of each child's development. It is also very helpful for older penpals to see at least some of the early drafts, particularly early in the writing relationship, so that they can write their own letter at an appropriate level.

There are multiple ways that the children can use the letters of their older penpals as support in reading and writing. The original letter from the older penpal should not be written on. Rather, it should go home intact, as the precious object that it is.

Photocopying should occur as promptly as possible, both after the letters have been read for the first time and also before the children's letters are sent. A volunteer might assist with photocopying. Once a volunteer is shown how the children use their older penpals' letters for activities and for composing their own letters, the volunteer will see how important the photocopies are.

If older penpals' letters are going to be used to support the children's reading and writing, they need to be photocopied. The principal needs to be aware of this factor before beginning the program, and you both should have a shared expectation of just how much photocopying will be needed. Each month, for each child, the most you will photocopy is the child's rough draft, the child's finished letter, and the older penpal's letter. Over seven or eight months, the maximum this would be is six or seven pages per child per month.

The Annual Review of the Program

It is invaluable to debrief at the end of the year to determine which things were successful and which things need to be changed the following year. Classroom teachers and penpal coordinators each bring a list of (1) successful or good things about the program as well as a list of (2) problematic areas and (3) suggestions for modification or change for the following year. Open conversation is very important at this meeting, with a recognition on the part of both parties that everyone is doing their best to make the program satisfying to everyone involved. If things are not working, it is usually a structural or procedural approach that needs changing to more accurately reflect realities.

If more than one classroom is involved in the penpal program, we strongly encourage this meeting include all classroom teachers and coordinators, because more ideas and experiences will be shared.

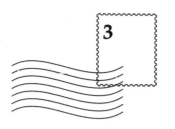

Preparing the Older Writers

Why Do Older Penpals Sign Up For the Program?

C.J. (coordinator): A big motivator for older penpals, especially at our university, is that people want experience working with kids. Many are either already in Teacher Education or plan to apply to teacher's college. The program allows penpals to really form a bond, because it is so one-on-one. The older penpals really enjoy that and feel good that they're important in this little person's life. Plus it's fun and cute to get letters and drawings from a child once a month. Also, some people continue with the program either planning or hoping to become a coordinator.

Older penpals should be able to expect, first of all, to receive regular letters from their penpals (although, unfortunately, this doesn't always happen, for various reasons). Second, penpals should expect to become important in their little penpal's life, and that they become a role model for the child.

I really think that it is the bond that penpals form that keeps the older penpals interested. Penpals should expect that there may be times when they don't receive a letter, but should also know that receiving the letter is not really the most important point of the program. Also, sometimes meeting your penpal in person is not as fun as you thought it would be. Kids who are really cute in pictures and on paper can be a different story in real life!

It's important for older penpals to keep in mind their position as a role model, and that they don't underestimate their importance in their little penpals' lives. Sometimes it seems like one short letter a month is not really that important, but to the kids, the letter is symbolic of their relationship with an older, "cool" person who thinks they're important enough to write a letter just to them every month.

K.E. (penpal, for the second time): I decided to be a penpal, because living in residence, you see the same people every day, and start to lose contact with the "outside world" — especially with younger children. I became a penpal, not only because I thought I could do something good for someone else (my little penpal), but also for myself. Both my penpals were children who had trouble in school. Their printing, spelling and concentration skills seemed lower than those of their peers. The children were, however, just about the sweetest and most enthusiastic kids I've ever met. It made me really happy and excited to see the obvious improvements that came with each letter.

I met my penpal from this year for the first time about a month ago. He was very affectionate and had brought his mom to meet me. That's when I started to understand some of his problems. Right away his mother told me that he saw a social worker and that he'd told her that his dad hit him on a regular basis. We were in a gym full of penpals, and I didn't know what to say. The child was still visiting his father, though his mother told me that was his own choice. Also, his mother is sick and was going in for surgery the next day. It really shocked me to hear this, especially since I hadn't been expecting it ...

Being a penpal has been a great experience. There are times when I feel lazy and I don't feel like getting a letter ready, but meeting the child and his mom has shown me how important the experience is for both me and him. The bond we have formed just from letters and an afternoon of games is surprising.

We have been delighted with the enthusiastic participation of older penpals. Still, we wondered why older penpals sign up, so we asked. As is evident in the two responses above, people become penpals for all kinds of reasons, and they are likely to have various expectations about the program and what it entails.

It is important *not* to assume that the older writers will come to the program with an understanding of the nature of penpal writing or the abilities of young children in reading and writing. Potential penpals need to know the nature of the commitment before they sign on. We have found it helpful as part of the recruitment process for older penpals to sign a contract that delineates their responsibilities. This contract makes expectations explicit to all parties.

We give our older penpals a small package of materials that includes a covering letter with the coordinator's telephone number and e-mail address, the writing schedule and reminders about busy times of the year for the older writers, instructions regarding the final letter, letter writing tips, a list of common grammatical errors to avoid, and the contract.

Responsibilities of Older Penpals

- *Write regularly.*

We cannot stress enough the importance of regular letter writing! When a child does not receive a letter while everyone else in the class has received one, the child may feel a sense of abandonment or that their penpal does not care about them. What may be just an oversight — a missed deadline — for the older penpal takes on quite a different magnitude with a young child. We cannot stress strongly enough how important it is to write a letter for every due date.

- *Aim letters at the child's level of readiness and interests: predictability helps.*

Many young penpals are reluctant or only barely emergent writers. This is often because they are young, are learning English as an additional language, or have a learning disability or other special needs. These emergent writers might *not* respond to every question in the letter from their penpal. Writing is hard work for them and takes much longer than a skilled writer/reader may realize. Regardless, these children should still receive letters similar to the ones other children receive. However, letters for the barely emergent writers must be aimed at the correct readiness level.

"Predictability" is an important feature in suitable writing for these readers. Letters from their older penpals should have a very similar format from letter to letter, ensuring the predictability of form. The child becomes accustomed to the form in their own letters, as well as in the letters that the class shares as a whole. This helps the child learn to look for certain kinds of information in certain areas of the letter. This is part of their reading development.

As well, older penpals can help their young penpal predict and anticipate content in the letter. Reading is easier for them when you write about one topic at a time. For instance, if you write about your pet, give several pieces of information about the pet, rather than changing the topic after only a sentence. The more the children can anticipate in the letter, the more successful they will be as readers, and the more self-confident they become.

Using illustrations as content and contextual clues is a common reading strategy for people of all ages. Older penpals can draw pictures to illustrate their writing and even if the illustrations are simple, children do use them to help predict what this part of the letter is about.

- *Be sure that all letters are delivered to the penpal collection spot by the due date.*

Penpals may have written their letters to meet the deadlines, but that means very little if the letters are not delivered to the collection spot by the due date. When older penpals do not deliver their letters on time, the younger penpals do not have a model letter to work from. Worse, they are affected emotionally — their classmates all received letters, but they did not.

• *Attend the penpal Matching Meeting in September.*

The Matching Meeting is when older penpals meet the classroom teacher, get a sense of the importance of this letter reading and writing activity to the child, and learn about the overall Language Arts program. If older penpals absolutely cannot attend this meeting, they need to let the coordinator know, and the penpal must find someone who will bring them the information about their penpal.

• *Attend the Penpal Days in the early autumn and mid-year.*

These days are extraordinarily important for establishing relationship between younger and older penpals. And, they are fun!

Any older penpal who cannot attend the Meet-Your-Penpal Day in the early autumn should do the following:
  – let the coordinator know of their absence;
  – find a substitute who will attend in their place;
  – inform the coordinator of the name of their substitute;
  – send a note for the younger penpal with their substitute so their penpal understands the reason for their absence; and
  – arrange a day the following week when they can meet their younger penpal at the school.

(**Note:** The substitute will be the younger penpal's buddy for the day, participating in whatever activities have been planned.)

• *Explain the discontinuation of the letter exchange in a specific "Last Letter."*

The young penpals will still expect to receive letters unless they are informed that their penpals will no longer be writing. And, the children need to understand why the letter writing is stopping. Older penpals may have been more important to their penpals than they realize. It is important for older penpals to express how much they value the relationship they had with the child.

These two issues can be dealt with in a "Last Letter," (e.g., "This will be my last letter ... because school is over for me."... "I've really enjoyed being your penpal this year. Your letters have meant a lot to me and I'll miss writing with you in this way.)

Program Coordination

Because our program involves eight different classrooms, it requires more coordination than would a program for a single classroom. In programs with more than one classroom, we find it is essential to have *another* level of coordination, including a *penpal* coordinator, a *senior* coordinator, and a *junior* coordinator, to ensure that all university penpals operate on the same assumptions. In our program, the majority of the following responsibilities fall to senior and junior coordinators rather than an individual "coordinator" for one classroom. For this book, we assume that you will be starting a penpal program for your own classroom only, so we discuss the role of coordinator in terms of responsibilities for a single classroom.

Responsibilities of the Coordinator

- *Assist the teacher in recruiting older penpals*

Oftentimes, the teacher will have identified the source for older penpals, but will not have recruited the individual people from that source. Because the coordinator is someone from within the source institution or organization, the coordinator is the person who helps recruit individual people to be writers. Recruiting older penpals can be done in a fairly short time span. Alert people to the program ahead of time, but have a sign-up period of only a week or so.

- *Put together packages of materials for the older penpals*

In consultation with the classroom teacher, the coordinator puts together a package of materials to assist the older penpals in their writing:
  - welcome letter
  - the writing schedule
  - two letter writing tips handouts
  - common grammatical errors to avoid handout

- *Penpal Contracts and Money*

Our older penpals complete a Penpal Contract when they sign up. The coordinator is responsible for collecting these. As well, our university penpals pay a fee (presently around $10.00) to cover the printing costs for handouts, the costs of refreshments for university Penpal Days, their own bus transportation to and from the school Penpal Day, and their supplies for writing letters to the young penpals. The coordinator is responsible for collecting the money.

If your source for older penpals is a business/industry, it is very possible that they might show support by covering these costs. (This would be an excellent community contribution, and the coordinator should pursue this possiblity.)

Many of the older penpals use their own materials for the letters, but it is problematic for some writers to purchase those materials. To alleviate this situation, the penpal coordinator purchases plain inexpensive paper, construction paper, markers, glue sticks, scissors, etc. and puts those materials in a central location so the older penpals can use them. This has been most helpful for some of the older penpals.

- *Match older and younger penpals and compile a list of the matchings*

The coordinator is responsible for matching the older and younger penpals. (See Matching Penpals, later in this chapter.) When the matching is completed, the coordinator compiles a list of the penpal pairs (including the older penpals' telephone numbers and e-mail addresses), and the coordinator gives the teacher a copy of the list. This list is used if the coordinator must contact penpals who are delinquent in their writing, or if the older penpal needs to be informed of special circumstances relating to the younger penpal.

We recommend that you also create a list of extra, back-up writers. If there are no extra older penpals when the matching is completed, the coordinator should recruit more "potential" writers. These potential writers are called upon if an older penpal is delinquent in their writing and must be replaced, and if new children move into the classroom and need a penpal. (It is often a month or so before additional writers are required, but we usually need several over the course of the year.)

• *Set up an e-mail distribution list*

Communication with older penpals can be greatly facilitated through e-mail, especially in a large institution such as a university. Virtually all university students have access to e-mail and use it often to communicate with their friends. We have found e-mail communication to be one of the most effective ways of communicating with university penpals. If the institution is a smaller workplace, an e-mail distribution list may not be necessary, as communication might be possible through notices posted where participants know to look for them.

The penpal coordinator sends a test e-mail to older penpals to verify the addresses. Our coordinators have found it helpful to use e-mail to remind older penpals of things like the deadline for the first letter and the date and time of the Meet-Your-Penpal Day. The most effective messages are positive in tone, encourage the older penpals, and emphasize how important individual letters are to the children. Older penpals also find it immensely helpful to receive information about what the children are studying or ideas for things to include in their letters.

• *Organize the Meet-Your-Penpal Day*

Well before September, the coordinator and the classroom teacher establish a date for the Meet-Your-Penpal Day. The coordinator then finds a suitable location for the meeting.

As soon as the older penpals have sent their first letter, the coordinator meets with volunteers from the older penpals to plan appropriate activities for this first Penpal Day. These activities might include, among others, a tour of the premises, where the children have to count the number of steps in a staircase, find the institutional logo, or identify and locate the mail room.

• *Ensure timely penpal letter exchange with the classroom teacher*

On the days that penpal letters are due, the coordinator collects them at the end of the day, and ensures that all letters are present. If any are missing, the coordinator immediately contacts

A point to remember: Many people, regardless of their occupation, can be difficult to contact, given schedules, work responsibilities, and family obligations.

the delinquent writers, encouraging them to get a letter in the next day. We usually allow two "slip" days between the deadline for drop-off at the internal location and the day that the letters will be given to the teacher. This gives delinquent writers enough time to get their letters in, so that every child will receive a letter.

• *Dealing with delinquent writers*

The coordinator is responsible for dealing with delinquent older writers. There are many reasons that a letter may be late, and we assume that each penpal is committed to the program and to their young penpal. Thus, the tone matters very much in how the coordinator approaches a delinquent writer. The first time that an older penpal is delinquent, the coordinator should approach the writer positively.

If a writer has been delinquent twice, we do not allow that writer to remain in the program (unless the reason for delinquency seems to be cleared up entirely). Two-time delinquents are asked to try again the following year; but, we stress that this year does not seem to be a good year to take on this responsibility.

Two-time delinquent writers must be replaced with a new older penpal. The coordinator contacts one of the people on the list of additional potential penpals. This new writer often needs to write a letter by the next day, explaining that they are the child's new penpal and saying how excited they are. It will be helpful if the new penpal can send a photograph of themselves to the child in a subsequent letter. As well, the coordinator can also get information about the child from the teacher and send it to the new penpal.

• *Organize transportation to the school Penpal Day*

The coordinator arranges the transportation for older penpals to and from the midyear Penpal Day at the school. This ensures that all the older penpals arrive at the school at the same time. From the point of view of the classroom teachers, this is very important.

The coordinator books the bus, informs the older penpals of departure time and place, and reminds the older penpals of this trip to the school. (Details of arrival time and departure from the school are arranged in conjunction with the teacher.)

• *Debriefing with the classroom teacher at the end of the year*

At the end of the penpal year, the coordinator and the teacher review the operations of the program. It is important to identify the aspects of the program that worked well; those that were challenging or problematic in any way; and to generate changes for the following year. We have found these meetings to be essential in the ongoing refinement of the penpal program. It is likely that each particular classroom in a new program will require its own modifications and adaptations.

Details of Matching Penpals

Over the years of working with this program, we have learned that the most important thing is for the older penpal to write regularly and to be truly interested in the child. However, we have also come to realize that just a little more attention in the matching of older and younger penpals can have some wonderful and unexpected results. There are two main things we have learned about matching:

1. It is important to find penpals for a whole class as quickly as possible.
2. If possible, matching penpals by sex, cultural heritage, or area of interest can often be very helpful — especially to the young child — but it is not essential.

Matching by sex is very straightforward and should be done automatically as much as possible. (Note that at the penpal Matching Meeting some switches may occur if the classroom teacher realizes that some matches may be more beneficial regarding heritage.)

• Fill a Single Classroom

In the past when we concentrated too much on trying to match people by area of interest, we found that the matching process was taking longer than we wished (sometimes as long as a month). This is valuable writing time. It is much more satisfactory to find penpals for all the children.

As soon as all children in a classroom are matched with an older penpal, all parties are notified of their penpal match. The older penpals begin the writing process by sending the first letter.

Your older penpal source may provide more than a single classroom's worth of writers, and you may be able to match a given classroom without using up your pool of older penpals. We strongly recommend matching the single classroom and getting its penpal writing process started — even if all the older penpals have not yet been matched. We have learned that it takes a bit of time and a lot of organizational thinking to work out the classroom routines. Getting things going for a whole class at a time makes it easier to build those structures into the regular program schedule.

• Matching by Cultural Heritage

We have found that when younger penpals can be matched according to cultural heritage, the older penpal is often able to play an even stronger role as a mentor for the child. This is especially true in urban areas or areas where one culture may dominate and children of less-dominant cultures do not see their cultures reflected, their traditions acknowledged, or their home languages spoken. When exact cultural heritage matches cannot be made, even matching persons who are both of less-dominant cultural heritage can be helpful. For instance, we found the match between a Vietnamese boy with a young male university student of South Asian Canadian heritage was so strong a match that the relationship continued for three years.

- *Only One Younger Penpal per Older Penpal*

Sometimes there might be "almost but not quite enough" older penpals for a class. It is very tempting in these cases to let especially keen older penpals have more than one younger penpal. Certainly keen older writers can handle the amount of correspondence involved. However, we caution against doing this. Our experience has shown us that the younger writers want "ownership" of their older penpals; sharing the older penpal with another child in the class takes something away from the whole relationship. Remember that this is a mentoring relationship, and the individual attention that the person being mentored receives is part of what motivates that person. This is true for our emergent writers, for whom writing can be very hard work.

The children's delight in having a single person who gives them undivided attention is especially evident at the times when the penpals get together during the year. And, although we are still doing research to discover more about these one-on-one relationships, we sense that the specialness that comes from having one person who writes only to them is part of what makes the writing relationship meaningful and motivating.

- *The Bottom Line: Get the Letter Writing Started*

This is the bottom line; however, we add this word of caution. Identifying the children's areas of interest quickly so that you can get the list to the coordinator can be cumbersome. It is much more important to indicate the sex of the child and get the class list to the coordinator. The matching and notification process at the other end can be more difficult than anticipated. The most important thing is to get the letter writing started.

Contracts for Older Penpals

Many older writers are very enthusiastic about the idea of writing to a young child and encouraging that child in his or her writing. However, without an outline of their responsibilities, some older penpals do not maintain the regular writing that the penpal program requires.

This is understandable, and it is the shared responsibility of the teacher and the coordinator to ensure that the older penpals *do* understand their responsibilities. These include:

1. maintaining regular correspondence;
2. attending the Matching Meeting and Penpal Days; and

3. ensuring that their letters are of high enough quality to be used as models by the children.

We have devised a Penpal Contract that has been very helpful in establishing the seriousness of the commitment promised by older penpals. Initially, we were concerned that a contract might be too formal and might alienate older penpals. However, those fears were unwarranted, and we have come to recognize the value of the contract for the older penpals. The contract we presently use asks for contact information and outlines the program's expectations of the older penpal. If you use a contract, make it in duplicate, or photocopy it, because the coordinator as well as the older penpals need copies. Our current contract is included in this book with the package of handouts for older penpals.

The Matching Meeting

The Matching Meeting is a very important aspect of preparing the older penpals for the "big picture" of what the program is all about and about their responsibilities. Meet with your older penpals as soon as possible after completing the matching. (For us, this is around the third week of September.) The coordinator organizes this meeting: determining the date and time with the teacher and setting the agenda for the meeting. The coordinator also runs the meeting.

The Matching Meeting is not held just to inform older penpals of the names of the children to whom they will be writing. It serves other equally important purposes:

1. to help older penpals understand the seriousness of their responsibilities;
2. to help the older writers understand the children to whom they will be writing;
3. to help them understand how the program is an integral part of the teacher's Language Arts curriculum; and
4. to enable the classroom teacher to meet the older penpals.

Beginning the Meeting

It is all right to dramatize this a bit. After all, when a child does not receive a letter, that child feels betrayed and devalued. And, probably, the single most difficult thing teachers must deal with in this program is a child who does not receive a letter. Use this opportunity to let the older penpals know just how important their letter is ... every month.

The coordinator begins with an overview of the program, stressing that the primary purpose of the program is to encourage the emergent writers. The coordinator also reminds the older penpals of the hard work that writing can be for many young children. We emphasize the importance of regular writing and describe how a child feels when they are the only one who did not receive a letter.

The coordinator explains the location of the letter drop-off and reminds the older penpals when the first letter must be delivered to that location. Penpals also learn why writing in conventional letter format is so important, and they are given a sample print size that is appropriate for the children to whom they are writing. Suggest ideas about what older penpals might tell the children about themselves in the first letter to the children. Encourage the older penpals to send a photograph of themselves in the first letter. The photographs help the children establish a concrete connection to their penpals. The photographs are also helpful in preparing the children to meet their penpals just a week or two later. Remind the older penpals to ask their young penpal one or two questions in each letter.

The Teacher and Older Penpals Meeting

The coordinator introduces the teacher and announces the actual penpal matches. This part of the meeting is the highlight for the older penpals, for they are very keen to learn about the child to whom they will be writing. If you as the teacher feel that a different match is more appropriate (e.g., the heritage of two writers), it is possible at this time to change those matches.

Next, we ususally have the teacher give the older penpals information about the Language Arts program, emergent reading and writing, and the children themselves. This meeting is a good time for the teacher to again stress the importance of error-free writing, size of print to use, etc. Some teachers also give their penpals a letter, reminding them of things that are important in their particular classroom.

As well as bringing samples of writing by young children, consider bringing along photographs of the children. This helps the older penpals write a more personal and enthusiastic introductory letter. As well, older penpals often put this photograph up in their rooms. Having a photograph of the child prompts the older penpal to send a photograph of themselves to the child, enabling both penpals to know who to look for at the upcoming Meet-Your-Penpal Day, when they will meet for the first time.

The First Letter: Tips to Tell Older Writers

The first letter is the beginning to the whole penpal relationship — and the most important thing about that letter is that it gets written and sent as soon as possible. In this letter, the older penpal sets the tone for the penpal writing for the year. It is important that the children feel invited into this reading/writing relationship and that they feel the excitement of the older penpal about the penpal writing ahead.

The first letter is also the model for following letters, in appearance and set up (form), as well as in content. So, it is important for the older penpals to follow letter-writing protocols outlined in the package they received at the Matching Meeting.

What to write in that first letter? The older penpals can tell their young penpal a few things about themselves and then ask their penpals several questions. The children can then begin their own writing by answering those questions, and asking a few more in return. In the first letter, penpals often ask questions about brothers or sisters, pets, and favorites (such as television shows, sports, and games). As well as giving information about themselves and asking a few questions, the older penpal invites the younger penpal to the Meet-Your-Penpal Day, which is hosted by the older penpals.

Older penpals can find specific help for letter writing in the handouts from the Matching Meeting. Some older penpals use the handouts when they check over their own letters before sending them. Many older penpals in our program have found these handouts helpful throughout the year. (The handouts are on the next few pages.)

Coordinator's Welcome Letter to Older Penpals

Welcome to the Penpal Program! Thank you for deciding to participate in this exciting and rewarding activity. For this program, _____ [e.g., university students] are matched with primary students in _____ [name of community]. You and your young penpal will be paired together for the school year, writing to each other through your respective school addresses.

Our Penpal Program is classroom-based, which means whole classrooms are involved, not just a few individual students from a class. Teachers integrate letter-writing and reading into their Language Arts programs and are able to monitor the reading and writing development of the children very closely.

Parents are very interested in seeing the progress of their children as demonstrated by the letters they have written over the school year. Most importantly, the children feel special and proud of themselves because of their relationship with _____ [e.g., university students] who provide the incentive and motivation for the child to read and write! We hope you find this experience as rewarding as meaningful as have other penpal mentors.

Classroom Coordinator: _____

Telephone number: _____

E-mail address: _____

Writing Schedule for Older Penpals

Letters must be placed [in the Penpal box located at ....]. To ensure your penpal receives their letter, it is imperative that you address your envelope as follows:

Your Name:

[University] Address:
Your Penpal's Name:
Classroom Teacher's Name:
School:

The following calendar indicates the due date for each penpal letter you are required to write. Please submit the letter on or before the due date by 4:30 p.m.

Day of the Week	Date

Important Reminders

1. Your first penpal letter is due on _____. Please include an invitation to the [name of institution] Penpal Day on [date]. Please send a photograph of yourself as an introduction to your penpal.

2. Both mid-year exams (dates:_____) and final exams (dates:_____) are extremely busy times for university penpals. However, letters are due during these months. Make writing your penpal letter into a creative outlet or a study break during these stressful times.

3. FINAL LETTER: At the end of the penpal writing year it is very important that you explain to your penpal why this is the last letter. Since our young penpals are in school until (date:_____), they may not realize that many university students finish school by (date: month only:_____) and leave (name of city:_____). Be sure to let your young penpal know how much you have enjoyed being a penpal with them this year.

Letter Writing for Older Penpals: Technical Tips

When you write all of your letters, please bear in mind that your penpal will use your letter as a model for writing his or her letter back to you. Therefore, it is important that it is a good model.

1. Keep your printing large and as legible as possible: many of these children are still learning to distinguish letter shapes. Print more slowly than you usually do. This will ensure that the letters are formed more conventionally.

2. Leave a good amount of space between words. This aids in "decoding" (reading).

3. Write as error-free as possible: the children will be using your letter as a model for their own writing.

4. Use conventional letter format:
   Full date in the upper right corner
   Conventional salutation (Dear ....)
   Paragraphing (This is more important than you may realize!)
   Conventional closing (Your penpal, Your friend, Yours,)

5. Write with pens which are photocopiable. (Darker colors are good.) Teachers photocopy your letters for the children so that they can take your original letter home and yet still have a model to work from at school.

6. If you like writing different words or different sentences in different colors, do so. (But, don't use yellow or other colors which do not photocopy.)

7. Make a copy of your letter for your own records. It's easy to forget just what you've written in the past; but, the children have copies of those letters and will notice repetition. (Not a good thing!)

8. Please send NO gifts. Not all children receive enclosures. Therefore, think about decorating your letter or making a home-made card instead.

9. Decorate your envelope and the paper. Use color, borders or drawings to brighten your letter.

10. Know that the children use your letters as models. They use the form of your letters, the content of your letters, and many of the same words from your letters. You are a mentor.

11. Keep those cards and letters coming: Children who do not receive letters feel VERY badly.

Letter Writing for Older Penpals:
Content Suggestions

1. Ask your young penpal two or three questions: She or he will use your questions for ideas of what to write about. (They often need your questions to begin their writing by answering them. Look to see just how many of your exact words they have used!)

2. Include one or two news items — something about what's been happening in your life ... your interests, hobbies, etc. (Younger penpals will often mimic this, writing similar things back to you. That's good, because your letter has provided them with a model of types of information it is appropriate to write about.)

3. Be sure to respond to your penpal's questions. Their questions are often more serious than you may realize, and they help to establish information about you. When you reply, try to extend your information (e.g., if blue is your favorite color, explain why).

4. Comment on your penpal's letters. Recognize your penpal as a person who has valuable things to communicate to you.

5. Remember that writing a letter to you is oftentimes a VERY difficult and time-consuming task for your penpal. Be sure to communicate your understanding and appreciation.

6. Talk about things which are appropriate for a child and of potential interest to your penpal. If your penpal is interested in things about which you know very little, ask them to tell you about those things — but be sure to ask specific questions. (Also...do a bit of research and find out about that subject. Try to understand the popular culture of children of this age.)

7. Include riddles with answers...age-appropriate jokes...write a short poem. Show your penpal how much fun language can be!

8. Use origami to fold your letters if you are so inclined.

9. Clip pictures/drawings from magazines and newspapers and glue them onto your letters.

10. Cut your letter into a neat shape (e.g., a person).

11. Word process letters and add clip art. But, be sure to use a font that is large enough (18 point for beginning readers) and spacing of at least 1.5 or 2.

12. Decorate the envelope to increase your penpal's curiosity about the letter inside!

Common Grammatical Errors to Avoid

1. The spelling of your penpal's name

   • We are all very conscious of the spelling of our names. Misspelling your penpal's name simply means that you do not care enough to take the time to be sure that the most important thing in the whole letter is spelled correctly.

2. Apostrophe errors

   • lack of apostrophe in contractions:
     e.g., cant [incorrect] instead of can't [correct] or its [incorrect] instead of it's [correct]

   • using an apostrophe when none is required
     e.g., it's instead of its

   • incorrect apostrophe with plural:
     e.g., holiday's [incorrect] instead of holidays [correct]

   • Note that "its" is the possessive for it; and "it's" is the contraction of "it is."

3. Confusing homonyms

   • e.g., your instead of you're (you're ------> you are)

4. Using "alot" as one word

   • It is spelled as two words: a lot.

5. Using "good" instead of "well"

   • School is going good for me. [incorrect]

   • School is going well for me. [correct]

PENPAL CONTRACT

Name _____   Gender   M   F

Address _____   Telephone _____
        _____   E-mail _____

Have you previously been a penpal with our program?   Y   N

Would you like to write to that child again this year?   Y   N

By signing this paper I agree to:

- Write my penpal once each month on the appropriate dates.

- Write my letters as legibly and error-free as possible.

- Send my first letter no later than [   ].

- Not send my young penpal any gifts or try to meet my penpal in person other than at the organized Penpal Days.

- Attend the Penpal Matching Meeting, the university Penpal Day and the public school Penpal Day. OR If I cannot attend, I will notify my Classroom Coordinator of the name and telephone number of the person who will be my substitute, and I will arrange a time to meet at the child's school the following week.

- Check my e-mail regularly for messages from the Penpal Coordinator.

I understand that if at any time during the school year I am unable to continue writing to my penpal, I must contact my coordinator BEFORE I stop writing.

_____   _____
Signature   Date

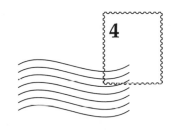

Preparations for Supporting the Children

Where to Begin

The children need to be introduced to the idea of penpal letter writing. The classroom and procedures must be organized to ensure success for every child, regardless of their initial reading and writing abilities. This chapter provides concrete suggestions that are very important in preparing the support structures for the children in a penpal program.

Responsibilities of the Classroom Teacher

- *Commitment to the penpal program is commitment for every child in the class.*

This program is about a community of writers, and the community includes every child. You may need additional letter-reading and letter-writing help for your neediest children, but every child should compose her/his own letter, even if someone else scribes or interprets the letter. You will be surprised at the writing development of some of your children and you will find that their independence and motivation increase more quickly in Language Arts than in many other areas.

Some children have an especially difficult time writing letters. You can help these children by reducing the amount of space the child must fill. It will help to make the task more possible for the child and will ensure that the older penpal receives a letter. However, these children's letters need to look very similar to those of their classmates. One idea is to have the children write their letter on a 12 cm × 17 cm card. The child can decorate one side of the card and write the letter on the other side. The card is then put into an envelope, just like other letters. Another option is to form a card by folding a regular piece of paper in half.

Some teachers have found that using a template (page 51) is very helpful for the first letter of the year. This provides beginning writers with strong support for the form and content of a letter.

• *Ensure this is an enjoyable experience for every child.*

Sometimes it is easy to get caught up in a skills-development mode of thinking. While you will find that the children do develop many reading and writing skills through the penpal program, it is important to remember that a major objective of the program is for the children to feel the satisfaction that comes from communicating with another person over a prolonged period of time.

Your initial assistance may be greater for some children than you wish. However, use your judgment to ensure that the frustration level does not become too great for your neediest children: Assistance in scribing and in reading may be the best kind of support you can give at certain stages.

In guiding your practice, remember Vygotsky's "Zone of Proximal Development." Novices need stronger support structures and assistance than do more expert members of the community. We work towards enabling novices to perform tasks independently — to demonstrate their mastery of the skill or ideas they are manipulating.

In our penpal program, we welcome all of our children to the "penpal club." We want them to have the self-identity of a legitimate participant. Children who initially need greater support structures will, over the year, exhibit increasing independence. The first step may be small, perhaps just being able to work at greater physical distance from their support system. Your patience in allowing and providing children the comfort level that they need will reap rewards later.

• *Ensure that every child sends a letter regularly.*

It is as important that older penpals receive regular letters as it is for the children. Without letters from the children, the older penpals lose a sense of who the child is and what kinds of things will interest the child. It is through the child's letters and drawings that older penpals gain a sense of the children's levels of development; but, as important, it is through these that relationship is built and a sense of caring and commitment is fostered. If a child has been ill or absent, it is important to advise the older penpal, possibly writing a short note yourself to include in the bundle of letters delivered to the older penpals. Then, when the child returns, have them write a letter in response to the one that they have received.

_____

Dear _____,

Hi! My name is _____.
I am _____ years old and I go to

_____

_____

_____

_____

_____

_____

_____

_____

• Ensure that the child's letters represent their best work.

The children need to learn that we publish only our best work, and sending a letter to someone else is actually "publishing" it. Part of your responsibility is to tell the children:

1. **Do your best job in writing your letters.**

   Younger penpals have a responsibility to do their best job in writing a letter to their older penpal. The degree of care that they put into their work should reflect the degree of caring that they wish to have in the relationship with their older penpal.

   There is some difference of opinion among teachers regarding what type of letter should be sent to the older penpal: the initial draft letter or a re-worked final letter. There are reasons to support both approaches. However, we encourage you to take the children through the entire writing process, editing their draft letters, receiving editing comments from you, a volunteer, or their peers, and writing a final letter.

   For our weakest-skilled children, we still encourage you to have them write in whatever form possible for a first draft. (Remember that these become dated examples of their abilities at various points in time.) Then, you will work with these children, probably scribing the text in conventional format and "under-writing" or having them print the same words underneath the words that you have scribed.

2. **Include a drawing with each letter. (Optional)**

   Many teachers have their students include a drawing with their letter. Incorporating a drawing helps teachers manage the classroom in terms of the reality of having children who are at different abilities of letter writing and it gives the children a penpal activity which they can all do more independently. This gives some children a needed break from their writing, enables others to move on to a task when they have completed their letters more quickly, and also enables the teacher to have children meaningfully engaged while they are meeting the writing needs of other children.

   This drawing can be of anything that the child wishes to create, or a picture idea may be prompted by the teacher. Oftentimes, children draw pictures of themselves with their penpals. The children's drawings are as special as their letters for their older penpals. Like the photographs of the children, these drawings often end up on the walls or doors of the older penpals rooms, bringing a warm human connection into the university penpals' homes.

- *Get a list of the children in your classroom to the penpal coordinator by the end of the first week of school.*

The sooner the penpal coordinator has this list, the sooner the older penpals can be matched — and the sooner the whole process can begin. Every day makes a difference in the beginning of the year. Even if your class list seems incomplete, it is better to get that list to the coordinator and add a name or two as they come in.

It is extremely important to update the coordinator throughout the year of any changes to that list, whether it is children who move away or new children who join your class. Older penpals look forward to receiving letters as much as the younger penpals. When a child moves away, the older penpal needs to be alerted. And the older penpal may well become a penpal for a new child who joins your classroom.

- *Prepare for and attend the penpal Matching Meeting*

This meeting sets the tone for the whole year of penpal reading and writing. Be prepared to tell the older penpals about your classroom, about how the penpal program fits into your Language Arts program, and about the children. The more information you can give the older penpals at this point, the better their letter writing will be.

In addition to preparing information for all of the older penpals, it is a good idea to ask penpals of children who need extra attention to stay a bit longer. This means penpals who will be writing to children with delayed communication, children who are learning English as an additional language, children with special needs that might affect letter writing or reading, or children who for any reason might be reluctant writers. Let these older writers know a bit more about their penpals so that they can be sure to write their letters at the appropriate level and so that they can give extra encouragement to the children.

- *Make sure your class attends the Meet-Your-Penpal Day*

You will need to figure out how to transport the children, and if a bus is needed, how you will pay for that bus. (The first source you try should be your principal: Most principals and/or school councils have school funds for these kinds of activities.)

You will also need signed permission forms for the children for this trip. Having at least one other adult is very helpful. You may have an educational assistant or parent volunteers who can join you. Do invite parents: They are often very interested in meeting their child's older penpal, and we have found that this early meeting allays any fears or discomfiture that a few parents might initially feel.

- *Integrate letter reading and writing activities as much as possible with classroom and curricular activities.*

Try to be aware of the things that the older penpals write to the children, and bring that information into your classroom community conversations whenever it is possible. The children learn many things by sharing this kind of information, and they also have an opportunity to be in the spotlight briefly. Every child has a penpal, so the potential exists for every child, regardless of abilities, to have this kind of recognition. In addition to recognizing the knowledge that the child brings, it recognizes the relationship that exists between each child and her or his older penpal. Community recognition reinforces the child's sense of self as a reader/writer and emphasizes the power of language in building and maintaining relationships.

- *Decide what kinds of volunteers you need to assist you with letter reading and writing.*

A cautionary note. There are many types of volunteers that you might use, but remember that the children will all be composing their letters at the same time. We recommend they do it simultaneously instead of composing them individually at a learning center. Research has shown that children use ideas from each other and learn from each other even from overhearing what others are doing. When children compose as a community of writers, they participate in writing through talking and listening, and through looking at/reading each other's letters. They learn to orient themselves to others. Overhearing helps them learn how to sound out words, select topics, and co-construct text that they may then write individually. Your need for volunteers might be reduced substantially as your awareness and encouragement of this practice increases.

   However, there are still children who may benefit from the additional support of a volunteer, such as children who are attention deficit or who need stronger support in reading and writing in order to complete their letters in a timely fashion.

- *Arrange the second Penpal Day at your school.*

This is held midyear and gives the children an opportunity to show their penpals their school, their classroom, and their own work. You will communicate with your coordinator about this day, but you and your children should be the ones to decide what kinds of activities are appropriate in addition to reading the older penpals' letters.

- *Compile the exchange of penpal letters, keeping copies or photocopies of both the children's letters and the older penpals' letters.*

Over the years, we have learned that keeping individual file folders for each child is an efficient tracking system. The folders hold the children's original first drafts (or a photocopy if first drafts go the penpal). You will use these for assessment purposes and the child will work from them in the future.

Photocopies of the older penpals' letters are also kept in the folders, so the children can refer to them as they write their own letters. It is impossible to accurately assess the child's writing unless you see what their penpal has written to them in previous letters. Children often appropriate words and phrases from their penpals. The file folder is the repository of the full communication between the two penpals.

(Note: If letters are received without dates, date stamp them before filing, so you have the date for assessment later. Also send a note to the older penpal reminding them to put the date on their letters.)

- *Report any delinquent older writers within one or two weeks to your penpal coordinator.*

Follow up on delinquent writers immediately. There are many legitimate reasons for not writing a letter, from personal illness to a death in the family. However, the coordinator needs to know what has happened. If the older penpal has merely forgotten to write, the coordinator can prompt them immediately. Ideally, the delinquent writer should get a letter to the child within days of being notified by the coordinator. If the problem persists, it is very important that you contact the coordinator again. The older penpal may need to be replaced by someone who has more time for the program or who is more diligent.

Preparing Younger Writers to Receive the First Letter

Primary teachers know how important it is to read to young children every day. Children can recognize the works of many famous authors and they develop an ear for pattern books. They love to hear, and can retell, many of the classic fairy tales. Children's own stories often reflect the stories they have heard. By sharing informational books, we help children see the differences between fiction and non-fiction.

However, do not assume that every child knows what a "letter" is or what it means to be a penpal. Explicit conversation about these topics can make a great deal of difference in how the program begins and in the children's understanding of the first letter that arrives.

Children are usually unfamiliar with letter writing. It is a form of writing that few young children are exposed to very often. They may have a vague familiarity with letters, but not all children will have written a letter. Before embarking on a penpal letter writing program, make sure the children get to see and hear lots of letters.

A couple of weeks before the first set of penpal letters is due, bring in samples of letters, envelopes, and other mail that you have received. Talk about different kinds of mail. Include bills,

In addition, Chapter 5: What to Do When the Letters Arrive will help you get a clear picture of the logistics, so that you can prepare the children.

Using Volunteers to Support the Children

Teachers in the penpal program have found it helpful to have support systems for the children in reading and writing letters, especially given the wide range of reading abilities. You may prefer to have those systems be part of your classroom organization rather than using volunteers, and many teachers in the penpal program do precisely that. However, other teachers like to use volunteers during this process. Older reading buddies (about four years older) can sometimes be as effective as parent volunteers — the secret is in the volunteer/mentor's understanding of their role. The same principles apply no matter who is helping the children. Volunteers need you to train them about what they should be doing. They also need to understand their role in helping the child become as independent and confident as possible.

- *Training Volunteers*

Avoid misunderstandings by having a short training session for volunteers. The volunteer usually finds it helpful to have an outline of their responsibilities, with a brief explanation of why you do things that way. New volunteers can use the following specific directions to support the children in their emergent reading and writing — directions that will help the children become independent reader/writers.

Preparing the Classroom

There are some material essentials and organizational supports that are important to have ready before the first letters arrive.

- *Paper for the first drafts of the children's letters*
  You might have reasons for preferring primary-lined paper or unlined newsprint paper. Either is fine, as are a variety of others such as conventional lined paper. Just be sure that the paper is in readiness.

- *Pencils and erasers*

- *Crayons, colored pencils, color markers (and border stamps if you wish to use them)*
  Children will probably draw pictures to include with their penpal letters and/or will make borders for their letters.

- *Paper for the pictures the children will draw and include with their letters (if you wish to include a drawing)*
  You want to think about what size of paper you want to use for this activity.

- *Envelopes for the letters*
  Some teachers prefer to use school envelopes; others prefer to have the children make the envelopes by stapling together two sheets of paper. Some also fold a large piece of construction paper in half and it serves as a folder for keeping the rough drafts, final draft work, and picture together. When the letter and picture are ready, the construction paper is stapled into an envelope, it is addressed, and the child decorates it.
  Do be sure that the children's letters and drawings can be easily folded to fit into the envelope that is used.

- *A place where children can come to you for assistance*
  Establish a routine for seeking assistance, and have a consistent place where the children can go for assistance from you in their letter writing. One good option is a table that accommodates three to five children. It is large enough for your neediest children to spend a lot of time in close proximity to you during their letter writing. As well, other children should bring their letters to you for editing assistance during or after completion of the first draft.

- *A mechanism for addressing the envelopes*
  Decide how you wish to do this. Some teachers like the children to write their penpal's name and address on the envelope; other teachers do this themselves. If you are going to do it yourself, develop a procedure that ensures the letters and drawings are with the right envelopes. (We suggest that you do not collect these until the letters and pictures are inside the envelopes.)

- *File folders for each child or a penpal letter binder*
  In addition to a "working" folder with each child's draft letter, you will probably keep dated photocopies of the letters each child receives and originals or copies of each child's draft letters (and sometimes final copies) that they write to their penpals. These become part of your assessment of their writing

development. (See Assessing Language Arts Expectations.) You can prepare the file folders ahead of time, as well as a place for storing them. Many teachers use a box or a hanging file system.

Some teachers simply keep a deep binder for the copies of the letters, with a separate divider for each child. This method also works well.

- *A mechanism for photocopying the letters*
  Photocopying has been discussed earlier, and we do recommend it. Have a strategy for photocopying the incoming letters once they have been read. The original letter goes home and the photocopy stays at school. You need the photocopy as soon as possible because the children should begin writing reply letters once all the incoming letters have been shared. Of course, the children may begin writing their response before the letters are photocopied. The crucial thing is to have a photocopy made before that letter goes home.

  We recommend that you find a volunteer to do this, if at all possible. Remember that students in older grades may be able to do this task for you.

- *A letter opener*
  Once you see the decorated envelopes from the older penpals, you will not want those envelopes to be ripped in opening. When you use a letter opener, your care reflects the value of the letter inside.

- *A bag for the letters*
  Both incoming and outgoing letters can go astray very easily if they are not kept in a single bag. Every incoming letter is taken from the bag, read, and filed, leaving the bag empty and waiting for outgoing letters. Any good-sized bag will do, but we encourage you to think about getting a special canvas bag that you can label "Penpal Letters." It keeps the process tidier, and the canvas will stand up better to the exchange process. Furthermore, a canvas bag is similar to the mailbags carried by real letter carriers.

- *Deciding if or how you will use volunteers.*
  If you use volunteers, train them to provide the appropriate kind of assistance. Volunteers need to know that each child should retain ownership of the letters that they receive and the letters that they compose.

Information for Penpal Volunteers

The letters that the children write to their penpal are only a part of our writing and reading program. Our whole program consists of other things in addition to this letter-reading and writing. We do some language awareness activities, including attention to letter sounds, phonics, and the meaning of conventions of written communication. Some of our other language arts activities include a writing workshop, writing whole-class experience charts, and individual reading of books. If you have questions about the direct teaching of language skills, please ask me. I will be pleased to explain how we do these things.

The letter writing and reading that we do in the penpal program provides an opportunity for the children to demonstrate what they can actually do, as well as to learn how to do new things with your guidance.

Our objective is to help the children become as independent as possible in their writing and their reading. Therefore, in deciding what kind of help to give, ask yourself what kind of response will help the child become more independent. This will help stop you from just telling the child what to do (which is what most of us do by instinct!).

Responsibilities of Penpal Volunteers

There are several responsibilities that are especially important, but they all come back to the single idea that we are trying to help the children become as independent and responsible as possible in their writing and reading of letters.

Your specific responsibilities include:

1. Helping the child read the letter the first time:
- Ask the child if she or he wishes to read the letter to you. If the child does, assist on words the child does not sound out. Do not make an undue issue over the child's reading: The idea is to read the letter together as fluently as possible so that the child understands the meaning of the letter. Your role is to support the child in enjoying the letter.

- Before beginning the reading, look over the letter with the child and have the child predict what the letter might be about and activate the child's prior knowledge about these topics. Find clues from drawings or designs; have the child think about any special events that might occur at this time of year or which have just occurred (like a big snow storm).

2. Helping the child re-read her or his letter:

- If you are working from a photocopy of the letter, have the child circle (in pencil) the words he or she knows. (Word detective)

- Then, as you read the letter, have the child sound the words he or she knows. If you think the child might know other words, just sound the initial consonant and see if the child can read the word. Circle any additional words the child can read in a different colored pencil or a pen.

3. Helping the child write a letter:

- Have the child find the last letter her or his penpal wrote. Re-read that with the child to see if there are any questions the penpal has asked to which the child wishes to respond.

- Ask the child if she or he remembers how we begin letters. If she or he does not remember, use the penpal's letter or the chart/poster of a friendly letter as a model.

- Brainstorm with the child what she or he might write in the letter. (You may wish to jot down some of these ideas.) Remind the child of questions the penpal asked that the child wished to answer.

- Ask the child how she or he would answer those questions.

- Encourage the child to begin writing those responses. You may need to remind the child what they told you earlier. (When writing is hard work and when one is concentrating just on forming letters, it is easy to forget other things.)

- Follow our classroom procedures for spelling.

- If the child has difficulty in scribing their letter, you may need to scribe as the child dictates to you. You may need to extend or clarify the writing through additional questions, but be sure to write the words as the child gives them to you.

- Once the child has given you a first draft, re-read the letter with the child, asking if there are any changes or additions they wish to make.

Remember: Children who are hesitant about writing are usually afraid that they cannot do it and they are afraid to seek help. Your encouragement and support matter immensely.

Responses to Questions Commonly Asked by Children as They Write and Read Their Penpal Letters

In response to common questions children ask, some phrases you might use to encourage independence in writing and reading include the following:

1. Child: "I don't know what to write."

   Response: "What questions did your penpal ask you?" (Then, encourage the child to answer at least one of those questions.)

2. Child: "How do you spell ...?"

   Response: (a) "Do you see that word somewhere in the room? I see it in the blue sentence on the experience chart / on the calendar/ in your penpal's letter..."

   OR

   (b) "Is the word in your personal dictionary? Let's look together."

   OR

   (c) "Can you get it started? What sounds do you hear?" (Then repeat the word so the child can hear it.)

   OR

   (d) "Is there another word that sounds like it?"

   OR

   (e) "See what you can do and then just put a circle around it. We can go back to it later."

3. Child: "Will you read this to me?"

   Response: "Sure, if you help me by reading the words you know." (Then, try to prompt the child by helping her or him anticipate what will come next. You can do this:

   – by looking at any pictures the penpal has drawn and having the child predict what the letter will be about;
   – by pausing at words that you think the child might know, giving her/him time to say the word. (Even our non-readers can usually read their own names.)

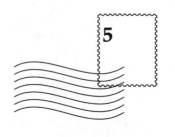

What to Do When the Letters Arrive

Distribution and Sharing of Letters

Twenty-one pairs of eyes watch as Kayla reaches into the large shopping bag, straining to reach right to the bottom. She keeps her eyes averted to be sure that she cannot be accused of reading any of the names. The faces of her classmates crane towards her as she triumphantly pulls out a letter and hands it to the classroom teacher. The teacher silently reads the name of the child to whom the letter is addressed, presses the letter against her chest, and looks up at the children sitting on the carpet. "The letter I'm holding is addressed to someone whose name begins with the capital letter 'A,'" she says. Abbie, Aaron, Angel, Amanda, Ahmed, Andrew, and Ashley are all on special alert.

The Basic Routine

The daily routine in many primary classrooms begins with the children sitting together on the floor for opening exercises. This is followed by sharing time, when the children share news or talk about an object they have brought from home.

In our penpal classrooms, this routine changes somewhat on the days that letters arrive. When opening exercises are over, we distribute the letters one-by-one, but share each letter with the whole class. Sharing letters as a community makes the strong statement that every child in the class belongs in this reading and writing community. Through our research, we have found out what really happens during this sharing process in relation to literacy learning. In this chapter, we will outline the literacy and classroom procedures associated with sharing letters.

As the year progresses, some teachers modify the process, distributing each letter for children to read independently, or with a reading buddy or other volunteer. In many grade one classrooms, this would not work until January (at the earliest), because there are usually not enough skilled readers in the class before then. If you modify the routine so that children are reading independently, we strongly recommend that you have them reconvene as a group in order to share the letters.

Looking at Things in More Detail

The general procedure above is enhanced by a number of language and letter-related activities. For example, when we pull out the first letter, we use phonics clues, and the children figure out whose letter has been drawn.

We also make sure that the children learn how to open the envelope without damaging it or the letter it holds. We ask each child if he or she wants to read the letter. Our role is to support the child throughout the reading. Sometimes a child starts to read the letter, but we actually end up doing most of the reading. When this happens, we have the child watch as we point to each word while we read.

When the children get restless, that is a cue that you should end the letter reading for the time being. There may be time in the afternoon to read several more letters. Look for opportunities so that all the letters are shared as soon as possible, thus allowing the children to move on to the next stage: writing the response letters.

Photocopy Each and Every Letter

It sounds like a time-consuming nuisance, but make a photocopy of each and every letter! You will use the photocopy for assessment purposes and for additional reading and writing activities in the classroom.

Letters should be photocopied as soon as possible. Prompt photocopying helps maintain the enthusiasm that plays a large part in the success of this program. Children will be eager to read their letters again and show them off at home. If you have a photocopy, you will not think twice about letting the original letter go.

Let a volunteer do the photocopying. It is one of the most important and helpful tasks a volunteer can do for you. Provide some guidelines to ensure the quality of copies. Each photocopy must be very legible. If the letter was written on standard size (8 ½" × 11") paper, reduce the size of the photocopy slightly to ensure that all of the print is copied. It may also be necessary to adjust the contrast (shading) on the photocopier, especially for letters with drawings and/or different colors of ink. (You may want to advise the older penpals that light colors do not photocopy well. If you notice they are using them frequently, send a reminder in a note along with the child's reply letter.)

Using the Photocopies

You can use the photocopies in a variety of ways that encourage the children to read and use their letter. Oftentimes, when the children receive their photocopy of the letter, they read and re-read it, sharing their letter with the other children around them. You can invite the children to do a "word detective" activity with their letters. In a word detective activity, the children read their letter, looking for and circling all of the words that they can read by themselves. This is an especially good task for early readers, for it provides an indication of the child's sight vocabulary.

Word detective is easily adapted (e.g., find all the periods, or underline all the capital letters). Older or more able readers can be asked to circle specific types of words, such as nouns, adjectives, compound words, or "-ing" words. In another version of word detective, the children circle the question marks on their photocopy to identify the questions they must answer. (More advanced reader/writers might circle entire questions in their penpals' letters.) The learning advantage is that the children are not only re-reading the letter, but are also looking at the format and using the content to shape the reply they will write.

Let's Get Writing!

Sharing letters usually proceeds without incident. Before the writing begins, we encourage you to have a clear idea in your own mind of just how the letter writing will proceed; otherwise, things can become chaotic. (Consider the pandemonium that could result if several children need assistance, and only one teacher is available to meet all their needs at the same time!) So, it is very important to concretely visualize just what you want to happen when your children move into letter writing. We have used the following methods with success.

• *Review the Model Letter*

By the time the first letters arrive, the children should be familiar with the concept of friendly letters. However, make sure you have a poster or experience chart model of a friendly letter on the wall. It must be readily visible to each child. Once the penpals' letters have been shared, draw the children's attention to this model, identifying where different things belong on the page.

What to Do When the Letters Arrive !!

1. **Open and share each letter with the whole class. This is done in order to**
   - include the child in the reader/writer community
   - ensure the children hear and see lots of different letters
   - to help children find ideas for content

2. **Ask the child if she or he wishes to read the letter. Assist as necessary.**
   - help with words the child does *not* sound out
   - make the reading as fluent as possible to ensure the child's understanding

3. **After reading the letter, ask the child and the other children to tell you about . . .**
   - interesting or surprising topics in the letter
   - anything they did not understand
   - topics they might respond to in their letter

4. **After all of the letters have been shared, have the children focus on their individual letters, in a follow-up activity. Try various versions of word detective:**
   - children search their letter for various features of grammar or written language
   - children can demonstrate their language knowledge

Even children can get "writer's block." Help them figure out how to get started by brainstorming as a group. Encourage them to suggest ideas for content. Ask children questions that will encourage greater detail and context for topics they suggest. And when they begin to write their letters, remind the children once again to check the model on the wall.

• *Using the Older Penpal's Letter as a Model*

The children should keep their penpal's letter next to them to use as a model for their own writing. Weaker-skilled children will need additional support from you or a volunteer. If you sit at a table that accommodates four to six children, one child can scribe the date while you assist another child. In addition, children can assist each other under your watchful eye.

The intensity and duration of the time that children spend on-task writing their responses can be surprising. Writing back to the person who has just written to them is a very powerful motivator — even for children who find writing difficult. When everyone in the classroom is working on their letters at the same time, the classroom is turned into a "penpal studio," and the on-task behavior of peers is usually enough to bring most off-task children back to their letters.

• Encourage Children to Learn From and With Each Other

During the writing period, we encourage conversation between and among the children, with the caveat that children still need to do their own writing or drawing. The conversation is often remarkably on-task, with children asking each other things such as how to spell words and where question marks should go. We encourage them to look at each other's letters to and from the older penpals. In doing so, they see several different models, as well as a variety of topics that they, too, can write about. In a community of writers, this kind of sharing is a good thing: It supports novice writers and helps them become more independent and skilled in their own writing.

• Letter-related Activities: Pictures, Borders, and Envelopes

We often have the children draw a picture to include with the letter. This picture is completely the child's choice. Children often draw a picture of the two penpals together, or they draw something they wrote about. The picture is an extension of the writing and also an opportunity for the child to work on a different but related activity. A drawing activity also gives you time get around to all the children — or for them to come to you for assistance and editing.

Other activities include making a border for the letter and decorating and addressing the envelope. Some children even *make* their own envelope! (**Note:** If the children's skill level is too weak, you can pre-address the envelopes so they are ready ahead of time.)

The older penpals' letters show children that many experienced writers use special stationary for letters. When children create their own patterned borders, they participate in the penpal culture in a different way. It also emphasizes the "published" aspect of the final copy. As well, by using *patterned* borders, you can integrate an application of the algebra/patterning expectations from the mathematics curriculum. For instance, children may be asked to do their pattern one month using an "aaba" pattern, or an "aabbccaabbcc" pattern. Some teachers even have a "pattern center" in the classroom, where children can create their patterns using pattern stamps.

• Use a Filing System

It will probably take the children more than one day to write the rough draft, especially for the first couple of letters. Given the range of ability in most primary classrooms, you will soon have several letters at different stages of completion. This is normal and should be expected. It can become a bit of nightmare if children don't know where their drafts and in-coming letters are. We find it easier to manage when we have an individual file (a folder or folded 11" × 17" construction paper) ready for each child ahead of time. The photocopy of the older penpal's letter is put in each child's folder for easy access at letter writing time. At the end of the writing period, whether or not the child has a complete draft, the letter and the older penpal's letter are returned to the child's file.

This routine reduces chaos and ensures careful tracking of letters. You can also look over the drafts at the end of the day, to edit or make decisions about how to resume the letter writing the following day. (**Note:** We strongly recommend that the letter writing fall on successive days; otherwise, the letter becomes stale and the children forget what they were writing about.)

Supporting the Children in *Reading* Their Letters

The most important thing is to make sure that each child understands the letter when it is read the first time. The letter needs to be read with enough fluency that the child understands the meaning and hears the older penpal's interest in them. If the child's decoding skills are weak, insistence on independent reading can be counter-productive. The challenge is to support each child as they read their letter, while maintaining the greatest degree of independence possible for the child.

There are several different approaches.

1. Have each child read their letter with the teacher, in front of the class;
2. Put children in reading pairs, strong-skilled readers paired with weaker-skilled readers; or
3. Have volunteers or older reading buddies read the letters with the children.

Our strong preference is for the first option, because classroom teachers are experts in teaching reading and they will be the least intrusive while supporting the child's reading. Equally important, this whole-class approach enhances the development of a community of reader/writers. The shared reading illustrates a broad range of letters and the kind of flexibility that exists in letter-writing rules.

By grade two, it may be possible to use the second approach with reading pairs. You may have enough stronger-skilled readers to ensure that most parts of the letters can be decoded between the efforts of the two children. However, older penpals use many vocabulary words that are far beyond even a grade two level. While we encourage the older penpals to be aware of the child's reading level, we also encourage them to write naturally and to use words that will stretch the children. For instance, our particular penpals often use the words "university" or "vegetarian" when they write about their own lives. If the teacher or an adult volunteer is helping the children read, these words are decoded without any problem. In addition, the adult can engage the child in talking about the meaning of these words. A peer or close peer of the child probably cannot decode these words, or they decode them without understanding the sense. This is not good reading practice. In our reading, we stress meaning-making as the most important aspect of reading. As well, a peer or close peer likely cannot prompt the child to anticipate or predict further information that follows these words. We usually discourage peer-assisted reading, unless the reading buddy is a significantly older and more skilled reader.

The third approach, using adult volunteers or older reading buddies, can be very helpful, but we have found that it is important for volunteers to understand how we teach reading and what *they* should do to support the child in that process. This information applies equally whether your volunteers are adults or older reading buddies from other classes in the school.

In supporting reading, our goal is to increase the child's independence in reading. We do this by helping the child develop reading strategies and adjust to the required level so they retain the most possible ownership in the reading. We also celebrate the child's reading accomplishments. The following sequence provides sound reading practices that you and your volunteers can use.

- *General Approach: Read the Letter Together for Meaning.*

Read the letter together as fluently as possible so the child understands the meaning of the letter. When the child is reading, assist only on words that the child does not sound out. If the child is reading too slowly, assist by reinforcing the meaning of each sentence after the child has finished reading the sentence. If you are reading together in front of the class, anticipate words that the child might know and have them read those words whenever possible.

- *Predict and Activate Prior Knowledge*

Before beginning the reading, look over the letter with the children and have the children predict what the letter might be about. Find clues from drawings or designs. Have the children think about special or seasonal events for the time of year (e.g., a big snow storm in December).

Doing this with the whole class models these processes and strategies for children who are still learning them. As the year progresses, look for children who are still learning how to do these things, and ask for their ideas. This legitimizes both developing readers and those who are already skilled.

- *Review the Letter*

After reading the letter ask the children to tell you about
  - what they found interesting in the letter
  - anything that surprised them or that was new to them
  - anything they did not really understand
  - what they might write in response to something in the penpal's letter

As a whole class activity, this models the kinds of thinking and active reading we want to promote with all of our children, regardless of their decoding ability. A child who is a good listener and thinker can contribute as powerfully to this kind of conversation as one who is more advanced in their decoding skills. It is important to provide an opportunity for all children to make these kinds of contributions, which legitimize them as active participants in this community of reader/writers.

- *Word Knowledge and Symbolic Identification*

Use a word detective activity after the children have read their individual letters. This works well when the activity targets the child's reading level. It also allows you one-on-one time with needier students. Depending on the children's reading ability, you might want to have the children do several of these activities, adapting the task to searching for different letters, words, or punctuation. (A note of caution: Too many activities done on the same photocopy of the letter will make it unreadable — especially for the children.)

Strategies to Support Children in
***Reading* Their Letters**

In supporting reading, our goal is to increase the child's independence in reading. We do this by helping the child develop reading strategies, by assisting them adjust to the level required so that they retain as much ownership in the reading as possible, and by celebrating the child's reading accomplishments.

1. **General approach: Read the letter together for meaning.**
   - You or the child read the letter out loud. Provide assistance as needed to support meaning-making.

2. **Prediction and activation of prior knowledge**
   - Look at the letter and discuss what it might be about.

3. **Review the letter**
   - Talk about the letter after it has been read. Ask questions, elicit comments.
   - Discuss what they might respond to in their penpal's letter

4. **Word knowledge and symbolic identification**
   - Use a language development activity, such as "word detective."

Strategies to Support Children in *Writing* Their Letters

Every child needs to be recognized as a person with valuable things to communicate. Your role (or your volunteer's role) is to help the child take as much responsibility as possible for the composition of the letter. Each child should decide what to write and physically scribe as much of the letter as possible. (If someone is scribing for the child, they should use the child's words.) Assist the children to write their letters, without doing it for them. For example, if a student is unsure of what to say, we ask probing questions to extend the meaning. We find that it is quite obvious when a volunteer (instead of the child) has composed a letter. This kind of "help" is actually interference, and it can cause real problems in the communication between the two penpals.

As we teach the usual features of the writing process, we make use of the intrinsic support structures of penpal letter writing. For example, both writers contribute ideas of what to write about, because both penpals are expected to ask and answer questions as they respond to each other's letter. Thus, both the adults and children must refer to their penpal's letter. Sometimes our support of a child is simply a reminder to use the penpal's letter for hints on content and form.

• *Basic Letter Writing Processes*

Regardless of the writing skill of the individual child, there are some basic letter writing processes that should be followed.

Activate prior knowledge.

Have the child look through the folder for the last letter they received. Re-read the letter with the child, emphasizing and identifying questions to answer and topics to discuss. If the child has not already underlined or circled the questions, it should be done now for it highlights questions to be answered during the writing.

Review the beginning components of a letter.

A child might omit the date or salutation. Ask if they remember how to begin a letter. If they do not remember, they can look the older penpal's letter or the chart letter.

Brainstorm with the child what they might write in the letter.

Remind the child of the kinds of things that the whole class discussed when letters were shared. You might print some of these ideas in point form on a piece of paper so that the child can refer to them later. (We found it also helped *us* not to forget them ourselves!)

Locate the questions asked by the older penpal, one by one, and ask the child how they will answer those questions.

We constantly remind the children to find the questions, re-read the questions, talk about the questions. It serves a purpose. When children can identify the question, it helps them to use the words in the question itself, re-working the order and changing some words as they compose their answers. Help the child to give additional information that extends their answers beyond "Yes" or "No." The answers should be in complete sentences. Explain that if they write just the word, "Blue," instead of "My favorite color is blue," their older penpal will not know what they mean.

Ask the child what questions they wish to ask the older penpal.

Remind the child to think of three questions (if possible) to ask their penpal. The questions should be meaningful. See if they would like to know more about something that their penpal wrote about in a past letter. Talk about what is going on in their own life that they might like to write, and ask their penpal about. For instance, a child who spent the weekend at their dad's house might write about that, and then ask their penpal if they ever spend time with just their dad.

Once a child asked two typical questions of her penpal: "What is your favorite color?" and "Do you have any pets?" The child had difficulty finding a third question and finally wrote, "How deep is the ocean?" This certainly demonstrated her knowledge of questions, but it was out of context. One of our intentions is to help children develop a context-driven, meaningful question-and-answer exchange in the letter writing.

Ask the child if they know how to end the letter.

If the child does not know one of the standard closings, look at the older penpal's letters or the chart letter for something that seems appropriate to the child.

Acknowledge and celebrate the completion of the first draft.

Upon completing their first draft, emergent reader/writers usually have a "Ta-dum!" sort of response, feeling that they have now finished the letter. They are understandably proud of all of the work they have just accomplished. It is important to acknowledge and celebrate this work before doing anything else.

Conference about the letter: Re-read the draft letter with the child, adding to or modifying the writing as the child and you decide is necessary.

Completing the first draft might be all a child has the energy for on a given day. This will depend on how much time was spent on the letter that day. However, as soon as possible, re-read the draft with the child, identifying parts of the letter that need modification. It is very important that the child has ownership over this; but, it is also important that you or a volunteer, as a more experienced letter writer, help the child see where clarification is needed or where ideas might be extended.

Be judicious in the number of changes or additions you suggest. For a child who has received considerable assistance, these ideas already should have been part of the process. And, a child who has been more independent will be discouraged if changes seem trivial or unnecessary. Writing conferencing is often a matter of negotiation, as it should be. Although your role is also to stretch the child, the final letter should clearly reflect the child's own ideas and stage of development.

Identify and correct major errors before the child scribes the final copy.

In our approach to the program, we feel that sending a letter is the equivalent of "publishing" a piece of writing. All published work should reflect conventional spelling and punctuation to the greatest extent possible. Once ideas have been clarified and modified, you and the child together identify errors and write corrections on the rough draft. The child then scribes the final copy of the letter.

You or a volunteer will need to scribe the final draft for children who are still emergent writers. These children can then write on top of what is scribed (overwriting) or write on the line underneath (underwriting) what is scribed. This helps a child who is still learning to form the letters of the alphabet be successful in their letter writing.

Different children at different stages.

Children who are at different stages of writing development benefit from different kinds of assistance. We have found the suggestions on pages 76–77 are of great value to volunteers and penpal teachers who have not done this kind of writing assistance before.

Strategies to Support Children in *Writing* Their Letters

As always, the role of the teacher or volunteer is to enable the child to take as much responsibility as possible for the composition of the letter. This includes having the child make decisions about what to write and physically scribing the letter as much as possible. If scribing for the child, use the child's words. This often means that the person who is assisting the child needs to ask questions to probe and extend meaning, recognizing the child as a person with valuable things to communicate.

1. **Activate prior knowledge.**

2. **Review the beginning components of a letter.**

3. **Brainstorm with the child what they might write in the letter.**

4. **Locate the questions, one by one and ask the child how they will answer those questions.**

5. **Ask the child what questions they wish to ask the older penpal.**

6. **Ask the child if they know how to end the letter.**

7. **Acknowledge and celebrate the child's completion of the draft letter.**

8. **Conference about the letter: Re-read the draft letter with the child, adding to or modifying the writing as the child and you decide is necessary.**

9. **Identify misspellings and other errors in language conventions and have the child scribe the final copy of the letter.**

Assisting Students With Their Response Letters

I. Early Writers

Early emergent writers often cannot yet scribe the letters of the alphabet independently and will need significant assistance with their response letter.

1. **The child copies the date and salutation from the older penpal's letter or from the chart letter.**

2. **The teacher/volunteer re-reads the letter with the child. This is oral assistance, and the child's responses are scribed for the child.**

   • to help the child answer penpals' questions in complete sentences
   • to help the child formulate questions to ask their penpal
   • to help the child think of other news or information to include

3. **The child then writes on top of what is scribed (overwrites) or writes on the line underneath (underwrites) what is scribed.**

II. Transitional Writers

Assistance declines a bit with transitional writers, who can scribe the letters of the alphabet and whose sound-letter correspondence is strong. These children will write their own rough draft using phonetic spelling and sight words.

1. **The child copies the date and salutation from the older penpal's letter or from the chart letter.**

2. **The teacher/volunteer or another child may need to re-read the letter with the child.**

   • early writers can usually re-read much of their letter quite independently
   • give the child enough time to decode on his or her own

3. **The child is encouraged to find question marks and attempts to read the questions.**

   • provide assistance as needed

4. **The child orally formulates answers to the questions, with assistance as needed.**

   • the child scribes these answers, spelling as best they can
   • provide assistance only as needed

5. **The child orally formulates questions for their penpal, with assistance as needed.**

   • the child scribes these questions, spelling as best they can

6. **The child orally formulates any other information (news, interests) they want to include, with assistance as needed.**

   • the child scribes this, spelling as best they can

7. **The child closes the letter, orally formulating the closure first if necessary.**

8. **The child edits the rough draft response letter with the teacher/volunteer.**

   • *then, if needed,* provide a scribed model for printing on a separate page

III. Fluent Writers

Fluent writers are fairly independent writers. They can do rough draft response letters with little assistance, using their penpal letters, word charts, personal dictionaries, or other resources.

1. **The child copies the date and salutation from the older penpal's letter or the chart letter.**

2. **The child re-reads the letter, with minimal assistance, to identify the questions the penpal asked. The child may highlight or circle these.**

3. **The child writes a rough draft response to the letter. They should include answers to their penpal's questions; their questions to the older penpal; and other news or information.**

4. **The child brings the rough draft to the teacher/volunteer for editing. The child may require help to extend their writing (e.g., more fully expanded answers, better questions, more context or details).**

5. **The rough draft response letter is then edited. If there are very few errors, the revisions can be written on the draft, which the child uses for writing a final copy.**

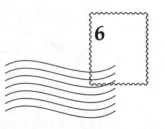

Ongoing Implementation and Troubleshooting: Frequently Asked Questions

In the ongoing implementation of the program, situations invariably arise where the classroom organization may not be supporting the penpal operations as you might wish. In this chapter, we have compiled and answered the questions about potential problem areas that teachers commonly ask in their first year of implementing the program. We have organized the questions into three categories. The first, Letter Sharing Routines, deals with questions and concerns about certain structures and strategies we suggest for sharing the letters. The second category, Letter Writing, answers questions related to both the physical and cognitive aspects of the writing process. The third category, The Program as a Whole, discusses other ways to implement the program.

A. Letter Sharing Routines

"Do you share every letter with the whole class?"
Almost always. We do not share letters with the class when the children have read their letter with their older penpal at a Penpal Day. Otherwise, every letter is shared with the whole class in the first months of the program (and often, for the entire year). If a child is absent, the letter is saved until they return, and we try to share it with the whole class then.

This may seem to be a very time-consuming exercise, but there are very strong reasons for sharing every letter with the whole class. It is especially helpful at the beginning of the program, when the children are first learning about letters and letter writing. When children hear lots of letters, they begin to internalize the letter genre (including letter format), topics appropriate for friendly letters, things to write about in their own letters, and the language of letter writing. These things increase the children's own literary expertise as they become more fully participating members of this reading/writing community.

With whole class sharing, even our weakest skilled children receive a letter "publicly," and this public validation of them as reader/writers does more to build their self-perception as a reader/writer than we can begin to describe! It is as important as building literacy knowledge and skills. The older penpal invariably writes of what an exceptional and unique person the younger penpal is. Sharing that sentiment publicly is evidence of the special relationship between the child and their older penpal.

Other children's reactions to the letters of their peers can be interesting. Perhaps the letter is Cory's; none the less, the other children are intrigued to know what has been written. (This may not be too different from the allure of reading someone else's letter, no matter what age we are.) Our experience tells us that sharing produces a very positive atmosphere for learning and community building!

"How long does it take to share every letter?"
It takes approximately two or three days to share all the letters. We tell students we will continue to share letters as long as everyone is listening. The duration of sharing time varies from class to class and from day to day, and it is dependent on many factors (time of year, day, week, and make up of the class). Scheduling constraints such as recess, gym, computer lab time, or library time can also interrupt sharing time.

Every year teachers are amazed at how long the children will sit and listen to the letters. They become interested in what other penpals have to say, and they remember and re-tell information from previous letters. If the older penpals use a certain kind of envelope, it is amazing how quickly the children pick up on this and are able to identify who the letter is from. They come to know envelope type, manner of printing, type of decoration ... all sorts of things.

An important role of the teacher is to ask children questions derived from the letters. Although this lengthens the letter sharing process, it helps keep the children focused, allows them to respond and be actively involved, and enables everyone to learn. When an older penpal writes about events, experiences, or objects that are new to the children, it provides a wonderful jumping off point for exploration of ideas, issues, interests, and cultural diversity. In this kind of sharing, children learn not only about the penpal's life and culture, but also about each other's lives and cultures.

"Do you ever feel that the sharing of these letters is wasting time?"
No. We sincerely believe in the value of sharing the letters. As letters are shared, children develop their listening skills. The letters themselves contain so much valuable and real information that sharing is a very worthwhile learning opportunity. Shared letters also provide opportunities to teach or reinforce many grammar and spelling concepts.

Primary teachers are always encouraged to read to their children every day, familiarizing them with various literacy practices and modeling the enjoyment of language. On our letter sharing days, the letters *are* the reading for the day. Our schedule on the two or three letter sharing days each month has two chunks of time for letter sharing, each about half an hour to forty-five minutes long. (We suggest that you schedule shorter periods initially and, as the year progresses, you will find that the children are eager to listen for longer periods of time.)

"What are some other ways of sharing letters without taking quite so much time?"
When time is tight, there are a number of other less time-consuming ways to share the letters but still ensure that children hear a number of other people's letters.

One approach is to distribute everyone's letter. The children read their letters first to themselves (or to you or a volunteer, if the child needs help). The children then read their letter to at least two other people, and share aspects of the letter together. The point is not only reading aloud, but talking about the letter. (Many of our penpal teachers have noted that due to the great amount of excitement, there is more noise at this point than at any other time in their classroom.)

If you use this approach, you may wish to structure it more (e.g., each listener asks at least two questions, or the reader must identify favorite parts of the letter). Also, if you share letters this way, we recommend doing it after recess, so it leads to a longer break.

Another approach is to have everyone read their own letter, with or without assistance. Then each child chooses a part of the letter to share with the whole class. This way, everyone *reads* part of their letter to the whole class, and ensures that everyone *hears* a part of every letter. Of course, these aproaches can only be used with children who can already read.

B. Writing Letters

"When the class starts to write their response letters, don't you find it rather chaotic?!!"
Whenever something new is introduced to young children, there is bound to be a certain amount of disorder. What might first be perceived as misbehavior, may actually result from a high level of excitement with the unusual. However, with the penpal letters, this high level of excitement is often accompanied by an equally high level of motivation. With proper planning and organization beforehand, you can lower the excitement level quickly and harness the motivation into some productive activities.

Children (especially grade one students and emergent writers of English at any age) often require lots of assistance with the first couple of letters. Everyone's writing needs cannot be met at the same time, so, at first, it may work best if only some of the children are involved with the actual writing at any given time. For instance, while some children are receiving writing assistance, others can be drawing a picture for their penpal or decorating the envelope. Use the letter template and put up a poster of a letter. They support the children but also enable them to be more independent and get on with their writing. The poster also allows you to direct the children to that model for support, thus freeing you, focusing the children, and providing a model of expectations.

"Do you use the same start-up letter writing process with grade two students?"
A few grade two students (like many grade one students) will need you or a volunteer to scribe the first one or two letters for them. We recommend scribing for a grade two student only if they are exhibiting severe language problems. These problems are usually associated with a child who is learning English as an additional language or a child who may be identified with communication needs (either at the time or in the future).

The majority of grade two students already have some basic reading and writing skills. In addition to copying the date and writing the greeting, they should also be able to find the questions their penpal asked. They should also be able to start replying to the questions with minimal assistance. The letter poster and letter template noted in the question/answer above, provide strong support and enable most grade two students to write their own rough draft. Few children in grade two will need the template as support beyond the first letter.

"Do the children always send a good copy to their penpal?"
Yes. We believe that whenever written work is going to be shared with an audience, an initial draft should be edited: Ideas should be expanded where necessary; conventional spelling and

grammar should be used; and the children's neatest printing should be evident. These features of the writing process should be applied to *anything* that is being published. In your role as teacher, you must ensure that the editing process is a helpful tool in teaching children to become better writers.

Printing out a good copy is not busywork, but rather a way to ensure that the content is interesting and, through the use of writing conventions and careful printing, accessible to the older penpal reader.

A lot of our older penpals are teacher education students, so the classroom teachers often include a photocopy of the child's unedited rough draft. The older penpal can see their young penpal's stage of writing development. It also enables the older penpal to celebrate the child's progress explicitly with the child. In these cases, the original rough draft is kept in the child's writing portfolio and is used as an assessment piece.

"How do you deal with long letters, when several students are waiting to have their letters edited?"

When some children have long letters, and other children are *waiting* to have their letters edited, you can have some students make a patterned border for their letter or work on a picture or envelope for their penpal. Edit only parts of a "long letter" at a time. When a section is edited, direct the student to write the final copy of it. When that is completed, the student can return. This helps to keep the editing line moving at a manageable pace.

It is often possible to edit the rough drafts of more capable students without their presence. Many teachers prefer to edit letters on their own time, using the next letter writing session to conference with the children, seeking clarification, pointing out any problems, and suggesting revisions. By the beginning of January, you will usually be able to do this with about half of a grade two class, and about one quarter to one third of a grade one class.

"What happens if a child does not have a letter to respond to?"

Any children who do not have a letter to respond to are still encouraged to write to their penpal. We suggest they ask their penpal three questions and give them two or three pieces of news. (Most teachers brainstorm with the class for ideas of news the children might share with their penpals, so even without content from the penpal to respond to, every child should have something to write about.) As well, children without a letter can refer to the photocopy of the last letter from their penpal as a model.

And we do feel that it is appropriate for the child to write about not receiving the letter — to voice their disappointment to the older penpal.

"What do you do when the letter from the older penpal is not a good model?"

At the penpal Matching Meeting older penpals receive several handouts ("Technical Tips," "Content Tips," and "Common Grammatical Errors to Avoid") from the coordinator. The teacher may also have provided a letter with suggestions on things such size of type, or the use of color. These guidelines for penpals are intended to ensure that letters of older penpals are a model for the children. If older penpals are using the handouts, they should not produce a letter that is not a good model.

Unfortunately, even with all these mechanisms in place, a child can still receive a letter that is a poor model. In such instances, go over those problems with the child when the letter is first shared. If it is a small problem, ignore it after that. If it is something such as illegible printing or poor grammar or spelling, write a note to the penpal identifying the problem and giving an example of what you prefer. Your tone in this note should be helpful rather than punitive. Older penpals often do not realize the importance of what seem like minor things to them. Usually, it only takes one mention of a problem to solve it. A diplomatic and helpful suggestion may be for the penpal to have a friend proofread their letters before sending them. (It is extremely common for people to miss errors in their own writing!)

One coordinator suggests, "Feedback to older penpals is very important, since it helps big penpals meet the individual needs of the little penpal, so both will have the best experience possible." Your support of the older penpals matters to the success of the program.

"What do you do when one of your students is away for all or part of a letter writing session?"

If a student has at been there for at least part of the session, send whatever is possible, with a letter of explanation. Sometimes a student returns just before a deadline, and time is very short to get the letter written. In that case, and depending on the skill level of the child, you might prefer to let the child dictate the letter. As above, it is helpful to include a note or letter of explanation with the child's letter.

If the child cannot get a letter written, send a short letter of explanation. Older penpals need to know what is going on every bit as much as the younger ones. Like the children, older penpals look forward to receiving these letters. The letters from the children bring the same message of caring and relationship to the older penpals as their letters do to the children.

"What do you do when a student does not want to write a letter?"

This problem rarely arises, but when it does there is usually a legitimate reason behind it. For instance, the child may be upset for not receiving a letter; they do not know how to get started; or they are having difficulty reading their letter. Once the reason or problem is identified and some solutions are suggested, the student usually gets back on track very quickly.

We tell the children that letter writing is part of our written language curriculum, and just like any other school work, we expect them to complete it. So, if the student still refuses to write after discussing the problem and some solutions, we then deal with it in the same manner as all other refusals to work. (That said, we have had only two instances of complete refusal to write, and both cases were students with behavioral identifications.)

"What do you do with students who finish their letter, picture and envelope before everyone else?"
These students can be directed to another individual writing activity. If you have computers in your classroom, students can write the final copy of their letter using a word processing program. They might also be encouraged to import graphics or to make a border around the page if they are sufficiently proficient on the computer. They might also be directed to an activity or project that is not related to writing or language arts.

C. The Program as a Whole

"How do you manage to keep the program going during busy times of the year?"
At the beginning of the year, when you set the letter deadlines, consider the busy times for everyone involved in the program, and plan accordingly.

For example, in one school, there were report cards and new curriculum issues along with the penpal program. The problem was resolved by reducing the number of letters and increasing the amount of time between letters — without going longer than four weeks in a penpal cycle. This kept the penpal program realistic. Letters were exchanged frequently enough to ensure the relationship and momentum would be maintained.

We recommend using a schedule so you can plan well in advance and so that you do not feel overwhelmed. Finally, the letter writing schedule is re-assessed at the annual debriefing meeting, and it is revamped for the following year if necessary.

"What do you do if some children get stickers and little gifts with their letters while others get nothing?"
The gift policy is spelled out for older penpals in the informational package that they receive when they sign up: Please send NO gifts.

Encourage older penpals to draw or trace pictures or to cut out pictures from magazines or newspapers instead of sending stickers. Some children will still receive some stickers, but children learn to appreciate the extra time and thought that goes into these other adornments. You can stress this in your letter sharing routine.

In one classroom, if a child started to ooohhh and aaahhh over a sticker, the teacher would reinforce that it was not the sticker that mattered, it was the letter. It did not take long before this became a chant!

On the other hand, if a child receives more than one bland looking letter, you might want to send a little note to that older penpal with some suggestions on how they might brighten up their letters. In some cases, in their letters, children just come right out and ask their penpal to include some pictures or decorations.

"How do you prepare your children for the final letter? Do they get upset?"

A schedule will help you prepare the children well in advance about when the penpal program will end and why. In most cases this has been sufficient, although teachers in the program are now planning one last meeting of penpals to say good bye. The feeling is that a more tangible ending is easier for children to understand than saying "good bye" in a letter. This last meeting may be a picnic in a park or zoo, or a final gathering at the penpal's workplace.

Some students who have established a very close relationship may set up something so that they may continue writing at home after the program ends. If a child or an older penpal shows an interest in continuing the relationship, it is essential for the older penpal to work through the teacher to secure parental permission. There may be many legitimate reasons why a parent or guardian does not wish a child to send or receive letters through the home address. The teacher is the most appropriate person to negotiate any arrangements. Parents/guardians must not feel coerced into continuing the relationship. If permission is secured, the letter writing is entirely in the hands of the older penpal and the student's parents.

"Has this penpal program ever been tried with older students?"

We have tried this version of a penpal program as high as grade four. A number of grade three teachers have also been involved on and off over the years of the program. The program was not unsuccessful; however, the motivation level amongst our penpals did not seem to be as high as that of their younger counterparts. There is not as much room for language growth through this particular penpal set-up for children who are beyond grade two and who have mastered the basics of reading and writing. This penpal program particularly meets the curricular expectations of children at an early stage of their reading and writing development.

Curriculum expectations for children in older grades are not addressed by the description of this penpal program. However, aspects of this model would be very helpful in setting up a penpal program for older children in higher grades, especially if there were a specific curricular emphasis for the program. For instance, some teachers of grades four through six have had very successful penpal programs based on shared reading of books, where the child and the older penpal read the same book and discussed it through their penpal writing. (The Appendix provides web sites for other penpal and keypal programs that might be of interest.)

"Do you feel that this program would work having your students write to another class in the elementary school?"
Many of the set-up and organizational procedures that we have already mentioned, can really only be done with an older population of penpals. Certainly, there are benefits to having children write to other children of the same age or slightly older, including children from other geographic areas or countries. A different kind of learning occurs in these programs, so it is important to know what your curriculum and personal expectations are for such a program. If your purpose is to learn about other ways of living and about global interconnectedness, the expectations may be well met if you connect with penpals from another country or culture. However, if one of your main goals is the development of reading and writing skills, it is not as beneficial for emergent or early writers to correspond with other emergent or early writers, because the children will not see and hear examples of writing from proficient writers.

Looking at Writing Development

The penpal program is an appropriate method for teaching writing development to all learners. The process we recommend supports literacy success and motivation through personal relationships and full participation in a letter reading and writing community. This social, interpersonal aspect of the program extends the literacy experience for children, by taking the learning beyond the frequently used forms of story writing and journals.

Advantages of the Penpal Program in Writing Development

• A real audience for the children's writing is established from the beginning. Writing and reading for meaning are essential features of writing and reading development. Children understand and accept the need for extending their writing when they have a distant but personally known audience who must understand the meaning of what they write. Throughout the program, the children apply their knowledge of language structures and conventions to create a meaningful interaction with another human being.
• Every pair of penpals takes part in an ongoing dialogue over the year. This dialogue is equally constructed by the child and the older penpal. It communicates personal experiences important to the writers, and is meaningful to both parties. As the relationship develops, each child has an ongoing, one-on-one contact with an older person, who serves as a mentor and support.

- The active involvement of older penpals and volunteers ensures the children receive assistance in reading and writing, at the level they need it.
- Children are highly motivated to write, when they know that in return for their efforts, they will receive letters from a person who cares about them.
- The format of the letters is consistent, which allows both less skilled reader/writers and more advanced reader/writers to develop. The children use the penpal's letter and the standard format as a starting point, which helps them to grow towards independent writing and problem-solving. The format helps more skilled writers because they can focus on learning to add details to their writing. It provides predictability and familiarity for less skilled writers, and helps them internalize the scaffolding structures. Predictability also promotes language fluency. The children begin to read and write their own letters by themselves, and they gain self-confidence and a sense of self-efficacy.
- The penpal program supports self-scaffolding and an increasing familiarity with the tools of reading and writing for all children. The children discover that they can use "resources" when they read and write — initially, by learning to *use* their penpals' letters when they write replies, and, later on, by turning to dictionaries, posters, sight words, and other people in the classroom.
- The penpal program can fit into any language arts program. A teacher can implement it without intensive professional development. The program is inexpensive to operate, and it brings the outside world into the classroom. It is a multi-dimensional strategy that facilitates the implementation of language development activities and that ensures the process will be meaningful and fun for the children.

Meeting Diverse Needs

During our time with the penpal program, we have witnessed marked growth in letter writing of students from a wide range of ability levels, with a great variety of needs, and in a wide diversity of classrooms.

• *Mainstream Learners*
Children entering grade one come with a wide range of literacy skills, knowledge and attitudes. Despite this variation, the most are mainstream learners, albeit at different stages of development. They can all benefit from the penpal program. In this chapter, we will profile some penpal interactions to show the kinds of writing development supported by the program.

ASHLEY: A GRADE ONE STUDENT

Ashley was a grade one student in a combined grade one/two class. She was quiet, shy, and hard working. Ashley was a strong and fluent oral reader, but when it came to written language activities, she was hesitant. This series of letters profiles Ashley's significant progress in her ability to use the scaffolding and in her actual written work. Ashley received her first letter from Alice in September, before the two had met.

Letter #1 from Alice.

Hello Ashley!

My name is Alice. I am your penpal. I hope you send me lots of letters and send me lots of pictures. I can't wait to meet you!

Your penpal,

Alice

Ashley started her reply to Alice by herself. She was instructed to copy down the date from the board and write the greeting by looking at the letter from Alice. She had some difficulty with the spacing, but completed this task independently. She had difficulty figuring out what to do next, because her penpal had not asked her any questions. In cases like this, you can remind children to think of the questions they brainstormed as a class. Ashley went back to her letter and made some additions.

Ashley's first draft illustrates very early writing development. Ashley put a great deal of work into this section of her letter.

Wednesday September9197

DearAlice

HODru ? I AM 6 e OLD

Wednesday septem
DearAlice berg9197
HODru ?I AM 6 eolf

Ashley put a lot of time and effort into this task. (Many first year teachers are surprised by how much work writing can be for young children.) Ashley was offered help in finishing her letter, and she was quick to accept. Ashley did not have ideas for other questions she could add. After brainstorming with her teacher, she chose two more questions, which were scripted for her.

After school, Ashley's letter was re-written by her teacher on lined primary paper, with conventional spelling, spacing, format, and punctuation, and space was left for Ashley to copy or "underwrite" the letter.

Edited translation of Ashley's letter.

Wednesday, September 24, 1997

Dear Alice,

How old are you? I am 6 years old. Do you have any brothers or sisters? What kind of ice cream is your favorite?

Bye, From Ashley

Ashley received her second letter from Alice at Penpal Day, where the two of them read the letter together.

Alice drew hearts in the corners of both pages of the letter and flowers and a sun with a smile at the bottom of the second page.

Dear Ashley,

Hi! How are you? It's me, your penpal again. Do you remember my name? My name is Alice. I am 19 years old and I go to school at Trent University. I am going to be a teacher when I grown up. What do you want to be when you grow up? I have 2 older sisters and no brothers. Do you have any sisters or brothers?

...e drawing pictures. I hope ...will draw me pictures when ...send me letters. I hope you ...aving lots of fun today at ...l Day! I hope to get a ...from you soon! From your

About a week after Penpal Day, Alice sent Ashley a third letter. Alice used differently colored markers in all her letters, with a new color for each line of the letter as well as for border decorations. This made all of her letters very appealing even at first sight.

All of Alice's letters were printed neatly. This is important for young reader/writers.

HELLO ASHLEY!

How was your Thanksgiving dinner? Did you eat a big TURKEY? I did! Yummy! [Smiley face at the and of the sentence and a drawing of a cooked turkey at the bottom of the page.]

ave no pets, but I wish I had
g or a cat. Do you have any
? What kinds of pets are
favorite? I like to play
s. I like to swim and play
ball, basketball, and
all. Do you like to play
? What sports do you like
? I also like music. I can
piano, the guitar, and I
too! Do you like [Page 3]
o you play nay musical
nts? Please write to me
m, your penpal,

Alice's third letter was not on the schedule. Rather than having Ashley respond to both letters, her teacher recommended using the more recent letter, because it had more questions to answer. Ashley was sent off to write the date and the greeting/salutation, and was then instructed to find all of the questions that Alice had asked. When a follow up was made to see how Ashley was progressing, Ashley had accomplished a great deal on her own.

Ashley is asking and answering more questions in her letters now. She accomplished much of this letter on her own.

Tuesday, November 11, 1997

Dear Alice,

I do not have any pets. But I like cats, and I like kittens. I was Bat Girl for Halloween. What were you for Halloween? [Page 2] I didn't have Thanksgiving. I didn't have a big turkey. I used to play basketball with my friend Kory. But I can't play with my friend [Page 3] Kory anymore. Do you have any brothers or sisters? I do. My sister's name is Jessica, and my brother's name is Thomas. Write back soon.

From Ashley

Note that in this letter, Ashley asks, "Do you have any brothers or sisters?" She already asked this question in her previous letter and, in fact, Alice answered the question in her letter on Penpal Day. However, no changes or additions were suggested to Ashley because she really had done an excellent job, both in the quality and quantity of her writing. Ashley was satisfied with the letter just the way it was, and copied out her final copy.

A variety of factors may have contributed to the dramatic increase in the quality of Ashley's second letter. When Ashley met Alice face to face at the Penpal Day, the two established a real connection. Ashley uses Alice's letter, which asks many questions, as a model. She also uses a comma correctly in the date and, even though she does not use any periods, she does use a question mark correctly three times. These uses of punctuation may be directly related to Alice's use of them in her letters.

Ashley demonstrates a much deeper knowledge of sound-letter correspondence than is evident in her first letter. Ashley's writing shows the beginning of spacing between words. Significantly, Ashley now writes three full pages to Alice about her own experiences (which Alice asked her about). Ashley also offers additional information (e.g., liking cats and kittens and playing basketball with her friend Kory). The communication is already meaningful for both writers as they begin sharing their lives with each other. In this regard, meeting each other on Penpal Day played a significant role in Ashley's writing.

Alice demonstrates good penpal letter writing form for Ashley by answering her questions. She also refers indirectly to information and interests that Ashley shared in her letter.

Thursday, November 20, 1997

Dear Ashley,

For Halloween, I was a witch. I wore a big, black hat. It looked something like this: [Drawing of witch's hat]

I have 2 sisters. They are both older than me. Their names are Susan and Heather.

I used to have a kitten when I was younger, but one day, she

...ery sick and I had to take ...o the doctor.

...ou and your family make a ...mas tree yet? Mine looks ...ing like this: [Drawing of a ...as tree] ... except I don't ...orations yet. I'm very ...or Christmas, aren't you?

Write back soon!

From,
Alice

Ashley has only one question to answer in her reply to Alice, which might help explain why this letter was somewhat shorter in length than Ashley's second letter.

In her rough draft, Ashley did not use any commas or question marks as she had in the last letter. We see that her understanding of these forms of punctuation are not yet internalized — not yet mastered. Although the letter is short, Ashley does respond to Alice's rhetorical question, "I'm very excited for Christmas, aren't you?" She uses a variation of Alice's words and she extends the response by saying, "I can't wait until Christmas." She then elaborates on this by telling Alice what she hopes to receive for Christmas presents.

Ashley demonstrates a degree of independence in her language abilities, for she responds using her own words. In her response, she makes connections between the text and her personal experiences, uses Alice's text to construct and confirm both general meaning and the meaning of individual words, describes her personal feelings, and discusses ideas and acknowledges a separate but shared experience with Alice.

When children branch out in their writing, they can take supported risks by trying on the words of their older penpals. These appropriations are not negative things: They are ways in which the older penpal's letters and voice serve to support the younger penpal in his or her writing development. Sociocultural theorists have taught us that this kind of novice appropriation of expert practices is a sign of healthy community. Ashley uses several appropriations. She includes Alice's smiley-faced sun (from Alice's previous letter) as well as Alice's closing from the November 20 letter, writing, "From, Ashley." (The closing was added when Ashley read the letter aloud before writing the final draft.) Ashley's letter shows her independent use of the scaffolding provided by her penpal and her use of a personal voice in composing meaningful communication with her penpal. These are both aspects worth celebrating.

Alice's next letter arrived in the new year. She continued her tradition of including a smiley-face somewhere in the letter, and writing each line in a different color.

Ashley completed the rough draft of her response all by herself, answering all of Alice's questions, and asking her four questions in return (two of them with question marks at the end!). In addition, Ashley writes the date and greeting in the appropriate place and includes a closing directly modeled on Alice's in the previous letter. Ashley includes a smiley-face, again imitating Alice's letters.

Alice's letter of January 13, 1998

Wednesday, January 28, 1998

Dear Alice,

How are you? Yes I have gone ice skating. I do think that sledding is a lot of fun. When is your library? I can't wait until April. It is my birthday. Do you have Valentine's Day? When is your birthday?

Your penpal, Ashley

94

The next letter from Alice was delivered on Penpal Day, in late February and the penpals read it together.

Alice's letter for February 27, 1998

> Friday, February 27ᵗʰ, 1998.
>
> Dear Ashley,
> How are you doing? I am fine, but I am quite busy with my schoolwork. I have lots of reading to do. Do you like to read? I like to read, but sometimes I have too much to read. It's fun though.
> I just took a bubble-bath. I think they are so fun! Do you like taking bubble-baths? They are fun when you get to play with toys in the bath too.
> So, have you been looking forward to Penpal Day? I have

> waiting for about 1 ... because I wanted to ... u again. Do you remember ... u came to my school (Trent ...) to meet me the first ... it's your turn to show ... hool. I can't wait! ... te me back soon. I ... iting! Hope to hear ... oon!
> ... r inviting me to ... t your school!
>
> From, your penpal,
> Alice ☺
>
> BYE FOR NOW
> ASHLEY!

Ashley answers each of Alice's questions and puts a question mark after every one of her own questions.

Wednesday, March 4, 1998

Dear Alice,

I am glad that you could make it. I have new shoes and I have been good. How have you been? What kind of ice cream do you like? I like all kinds of ice cream. Sometimes I like chocolate ice cream, and sometimes I do not. I like to go swimming in summer. Do you like to go swimming? And I like Minnie and Mickey Mouse and my favorite stuffy is Wake Up Buttercup. What is your favorite stuffy? Yes I like to read, and yes I like to take bubble baths and I have been looking forward to Penpal Day. Yes I remember that day. Bye for now Alice,

From Ashley

> Wednesday March 4, 1998.
> Dear Alice
> i am Glade that you code M...
> it and i have now toes and i have been
> Jode how have you been wet cond
> of ice cream do you like i like all conds
> of ice cream a saptimes and somies
> i like chok-it ice cream and i like
> to go swiming in summer do you like
> to go swiming? and i like miney and
> mikey mous and my favrit stufey is
> wak up Budrcup wet favrit stfey is
> stfey do you like? yes i like to read
> and i have been looking forwat to Penpal Jay

> Yes i remember that Day ...

This letter includes a lot of news/information in a fairly sophisticated conversational style. There is an energy to this letter that seems to reflect not only Alice's previous letter, but also the fact that the two penpals have just spent time together again, this time at Ashley's school. The affective aspects of this pair of letters shows the development of their relationship over time. Alice talks about how eager she is to see Ashley again, and asks if Ashley remembers when they first met. Ashley appropriates Alice's words, "Yes, I remember that day," but the response resonates with shared memories.

Thursday, March 19th, 1998.

Dear Ashley,
Wow! You have new shoes! I bet they are really pretty! I have been good too, but I am very busy with school. I like strawberry ice cream but lots of it makes it hard to swallow – my mouth gets too cold!
I love to go swimming in the summer when it is hot outside.

My favourite stuffy is my bunny rabbit. I sleep with him every night. This will be my last penpal letter to you this year because school for me ends in April. So I won't be writing to you anymore. Maybe next year I will be your penpal again. Do you like that idea? Maybe! I hope you have a great

summer, and I hope you have fun for the rest of your school year! Do lots of work, and read lots of books too! I hope to talk to you later! It was really fun being your penpal. Bye for now Ashley!
Love,
your penpal,
Alice

Bye Ashley!

Alice responds in a warm manner to Ashley's statements and questions. She picks up Ashley's topics and extends them. Alice also indicates that this will be her last letter, and she offers a continuation of the friendship the following year. She signs her final letter, "Love, your penpal, Alice." In keeping with her usual pattern, she includes a smiley-faced sun, this time, with the words, "Bye Ashley!"

In her own final letter, Ashley's voice is strong. On her rough draft, she wrote the date and drew a smiley-face that says "Bye Alice." (However, she erased that.) Ashley's rough draft has no punctuation except in the date. She may well have been focusing her attention on the compositional "meaning" aspects of the communication. (If we wanted to know about Ashley's command of punctuation, we would ask her to put in punctuation as her next step in the writing process.) In the final copy, she uses the proper punctuation, greeting, and closing (which she, again, models after Alice's).

Friday, March 27, 1998

Dear Alice,

*Yes I think that is a great idea. I
am having a birthday at the
YMCA and we are going to swim
there and I am going to have
peanut butter and jelly
sandwiches. Me and my sister do
not like each other and sometimes
we like each other. My favorite
part of penpal day was playing
outside and I liked when we had
snacks too. Thank you for being
my penpal. I hope that we can be
penpals too.*

Your penpal, Ashley

The differences between Ashley's first letter and her final letter
are quite dramatic. Her written language has developed to a point
where it better reflects her reading and oral language abilities.
Ashley has a stronger control of the physical act of writing. The
size of her printing is smaller and relatively consistent. Ashley is
even experimenting with "fancy" printing, in the closing and with
her signature. But, what is most striking, is the writing voice that
has emerged and the strongly dialogic nature of the writing (a
characteristic that is particularly encouraged and supported by
penpal letter writing). These kinds of results are not unique to
Ashley; rather, Ashley's development is typical of other
mainstream six-year-olds in the penpal program.

• Children with Learning Difficulties

Throughout our involvement in the penpal program, we have
witnessed the positive effects this program has on children with
special needs (no matter what their learning difficulties). The highly
structured format of the program is well-suited to this population of
learners because it provides them with all the necessary tools to
enable them to become letter writers. Programming suggestions for
working with students with learning difficulties are the same as
those given for students who are learning English as an additional
language.

The structures and strategies used with mainstream learners
provide strong scaffolding for children with special needs. One of
the major hurdles with students with special needs is to convince
them that they *can* write. Once they get over their fear, much
growth can be realized. And, with even just a bit of writing,
children with special needs receive positive feedback from their
older penpal each time they write. We cannot overestimate the
importance of this relationship in the mentoring and ongoing
affective support that they receive.

As with mainstream learners, it is important that students with
special needs, or students who are learning English as an additional
language, become familiar with the idea of letter writing.
Transitions for these children are especially important. In order for

them not to be frightened of new expectations, they need to have plenty of time to become comfortable with what will happen.

Introduce the children to letters through reading stories and by sharing actual letters. Children with special needs, or who are learning English, may need extra time with real letters, looking at them and talking about them. The books suggested in Chapter 4 will help the children come to understand the dialogic, back-and-forth nature of letter writing and penpals. These activities are designed to promote the "rituals" of penpal letter writing, such as the expectation that when they send a letter they will also receive one in return. And, that whoever receives a letter has a responsibility to write a letter in reply.

Children whose English proficiency is weak may need an interpreter at this stage: It is very important that they, too, understand the "big picture" of penpal letter writing. If possible, it is ideal if someone who speaks the child's first language can read one or two of the penpal story books to them, providing the opportunity for the children to talk about the concepts around penpal writing in their first language if necessary. This way, children still learning English share in the construction of what they will be doing in the penpal program.

Opening and sharing penpals letters as an entire class is especially important for children with special needs and children who are not yet proficient in English. Pause every now and then to talk about a certain part of the letter at hand to reinforce the basic structure of a friendly letter and to ensure that children who are less proficient in English are following along. Do as much as you can to involve them in the conversation.

Like children with learning challenges, children learning English as a second language are especially fearful of taking risks in any form of written language. These students seem to perform best when they are surrounded by lots of structure and support. The penpal letter writing format is an ideal vehicle to provide these things and to have them experience success in writing.

The predictable structure of the letter and the sequence in writing the letter help to alleviate the stress and fear that non-mainstream learners often experience. Using a chart or poster model ensures that these students *always* have something right at hand to refer to as they decide what to say and how to write it. (All the children benefit from the question–answer format in the penpal letters because they can use many of their penpal's words. This is especially true for special needs and ESL students.) Their penpal's letter is not only a model, but also serves as a kind of map, helping the children to see what comes next, and keeping them headed in the right direction.

An individual child's English language ability combined with their anxiety level will help determine the amount of assistance that the student needs. From day one, they need to know they are part of a very safe and supportive learning environment. Emphasize that it is all right to make mistakes, and that someone is there to help them when this occurs. In order to accept that nothing terrible will happen if they need help, some children who are learning English may need to observe other children making mistakes, seeking help, and receiving support. They also need continual encouragement and support to take those risks. Depending on a child's English language proficiency, they might need a "Big Buddy" from an older classroom, or an adult volunteer, to work with them one-on-one in their letter writing. This provides the close physical proximity these children often need in order to keep them focused, to help them find words in their penpal's letter, and to ensure they have the security they need.

All the children in the class should become aware of the wide range of abilities and rates of development among their classmates. Young learners are required to meet many various learning expectations. Relieving the feeling of competition here will enhance the reading/writing environment. We teach our children to be supportive of each other. You can explain that "Everyone is not reading or writing at the same level because we all learn differently, and we all come from a variety of different backgrounds. Therefore, we must never compare ourselves to anyone else, but just try to do our very best, and look for the growth within ourselves." Each child's own penpal folder will help demonstrate their growth, so that you can help them see it. Children who are learning English as a second or additional language especially need to feel both their growth and their legitimate place in the classroom community. Their involvement in the penpal program can go a long way in helping to achieve both of those goals.

MATTHEW: A PROFILE OF A STUDENT WITH LEARNING DIFFICULTIES

Matthew was a grade two student who had oral language and language processing difficulties. He was a very quiet and shy student, who was fearful of taking risks. Matthew first heard his letter from his penpal when it was shared with the entire class.

Mark's first letter.

September 18th 1997

Hey Matthew,

How are you doing? I am doing great! Do you like sports? I love sports. I like to play basketball with my sister. Do you have any brothers or sisters? I cannot wait to meet you or hear from you!

Your Pal,
Mark

Matthew and his teacher did a one-on-one re-reading after the whole class sharing. His teacher pointed to each word as it was read. Then she directed him to locate the date, and together they circled the question marks so that they could be found easily for writing the response letter and answering questions.

Mark's letter approaches Matthew as a person — not as a person with special needs. He provides the same kind of information that other children receive and initiates the idea of sharing jokes, something that is probably quite unusual for Matthew.

The children began their reply letters immediately. Matthew needed a great deal of assistance to get through the process step by step. He used the program's scaffolding by copying the greeting from the classroom poster of a friendly letter. Matthew re-located the questions in Mark's letter by finding the circled question marks. Matthew and his teacher worked together to formulate answers orally. Matthew needed a lot of help to produce complete sentences on his draft.

When Matthew had filled an entire page, his fatigue was evident. The rest of the letter was then dictated to his teacher, and she provided assistance for extension and complete sentence formation. Mark's postscript provided the opportunity to discuss jokes. With great assistance, Matthew formulated two questions for Mark, before adding the closing. Then Matthew underwrote his final copy.

When Matthew had filled an entire page, his fatigue was evident. The rest of the letter was dictated.

Wednesday September 24, 1997

Dear Mark,

I am fine. Yes I play sports. I play soccer and hockey. I have one sister and three brothers. My favorite color is blue. Knock, Knock. Who's there? Joke. Joke who? I joked you! Where do sheep go to get their hair cut? Do you have any pets? Write back soon from Matthew.

Matthew received his second letter from Mark at Penpal Day when they read the letter together. Matthew's reading level was apparent to Mark immediately. (Knowing the child's reading level can be immensely helpful to older penpals when they write their next letters.)

Mark's second letter to Matthew

October 3rd 1997

Hello Matt, How is school going? I am having so much fun here meeting new friends like you. I cannot wait for penpal day. What are you doing for Thanksgiving? I am going home to visit family. I hope you're having fun.

Your Pal: Mark

P.S. Q: What do you call an amusement ride for ghosts? A: A ghoster coaster.

About two weeks later, Matthew received this third letter from Mark. (The letter "J" was in blue.)

October 16, 1997

Hello Matthew, J   Look: A Blue Jay I hope you had a great Thanksgiving. I did, I ate a lot of food. What did you eat? Did you have family over? My grandparents and my aunt and uncle came over to my house. Are you having fun at school? Hockey season has started, Go Leaf's! I can't wait to read another one of your letters!

Mark

Written language is a struggle for Matthew, so Mark's playfulness both with jokes and puns is a rare event and helps Matthew understand how language can be fun. As well, Mark's exclamatory, "Go Leafs!" (a direct reference to the Toronto Maple Leafs hockey team) continues to build relationship with Matthew as a person — not as a child with learning challenges. Mark's closing, "I can't wait to read another one of your letters!" is an explicit declaration of his enjoyment of this relationship with Matthew, and it provides strong incentive and motivation for Matthew to write back to him, regardless of the challenge that task presents.

With everyone in the class writing their own response letters, Matthew was convinced to try, too. Sitting right beside the teacher at the round table, he received the considerable assistance and encouragement that he needed in every step of his writing. He began with the greeting, but was reminded to copy the date from the board.

The first part of the letter was read to Matthew. The word detective called for circled question marks. The word "Thanksgiving" was underlined so Matthew could find it for his response. Discussion about what Matthew did for Thanksgiving produced a collaboratively composed answer. Matthew was encouraged to scribe these sentences by sounding them out, by copying words from Mark's letter, or by finding them in other locations in the classroom. This was a slow word-by-word process. Matthew responded, "We went to wndes four Thanks givins. No one kam ovr." Mark's final question was located, and the words "having fun at school" were underlined for Matthew. His answer was again a collaborative oral response, which he then scribed, directly copying the second set of underlined words from Mark's letter.

The rest of Mark's letter was then re-read. Matthew and his teacher discussed some news or information to tell Mark. Again this was a slow, labored, word-by-word task for Matthew. He was most determined and wanted to write more. He managed the rest of the letter with minimal assistance. After completing the first draft, Matthew used a scribed model in conventional format for underwriting the letters immediately below the model printing. This whole process took about three or four writing sessions.

Matthew's rough draft.

Tuesday November 11, 1997

Hello Mark,

We went to Wendy's for Thanksgiving. No one came over. Yes I am having fun at school. I like math. I like the Leafs too! Do you play hockey and soccer? Do you like books?

Write back, from Matthew

Dear Matthew
How are you doing? I am great!
On Hallowe'en I was a mad
scientist. What were you? Did
you get lot's of candy? I do like
to play both hockey and soccer. I
will write you again before
Christmas. Mark

The usual sharing and partnered re-reading preceded the writing of response letters. Again, Matthew sat right beside his teacher to write his rough draft. But this time, Matthew copied down the date and wrote the greeting all by himself!

As Mark's letter was read through with his teacher, question by question, Matthew formulated an answer to each one. He needed some editing assistance for grammar or incomplete thoughts. He was then encouraged to write his answer on the paper. The process did not seem to be as slow and labored. Then, with little assistance, Matthew thought of and wrote three questions/sentences.

It was about mid-point in the program, so Matthew had heard and seen many letters. He had begun to internalize the format of the penpal letter, and now knew where to look for the spelling of words he wanted to use. These strategies made a significant difference to Matthew. Despite his learning challenges, Matthew was becoming increasingly independent in his letter writing.

Even in his first draft, Matthew demonstrated an awareness of some of the uses of punctuation. He did not use question marks, but he did use periods twice. As well, he inserts a comma in the date, and he was aware of the apostrophe in Mark's (mis)spelling of words. Although Matthew's use of punctuation is not consistent within letters, his use of periods across letters shows that he is beginning to internalize this concept.

Matthew is answering Mark's questions and asking his own, demonstrating that he is learning to use the format of the letter in his writing.

Wednesday, December 3, 1997

Dear Mark,

I am good. On Halloween I was a robot. I got lots of candy. Do you like baseball? Do you like Christmas? Do you have a cat?

From your penpal, Matthew

wednesday December 3, 1997
Dear mark
I am gn on Hallowe en
I was a robr I got
lot's of candy
do you like base bal. and
you like christmas and
you got cat.

January 15, 1998

To Matthew

There sure is a lot of snow outside right now! Do you like snow? I do, it's fun to play in. Do you like snow people? I think I will make one today. I would also like to go sledding. Have you ever gone sledding down a really big hill?

Mark

P.S. I have 8 cat's and 3 dogs!

In addition to copying the date and using Mark's greeting as a model, Matthew found all of the questions in this letter by himself! This was a major accomplishment. Matthew read over the questions with assistance, and he then composed and scribed responses with minimal help.

Matthew was now *really* using Mark's letter to find the words he needed to answer the questions. As well, he adds to the original question, not just writing, "I do like snow" but rather, "Yes I do like snow." An edited and grammatically corrected copy of the letter was scribed for Matthew, but instead of scribing underneath those words, Matthew copied the letter on a separate piece of paper, using it as a model.

An invitation for Mark to attend the Penpal Day at the school was also enclosed with this letter from Matthew.

Wednesday, January 28, 1998

To Mark,

Yes I do like the snow. Yes I do like snow people. No, I never went down a big hill. When is your birthday? My birthday is February 20. Do you like the Mighty Ducks? Do you like the Raptors? I lost my hockey game four to three.

From Matthew

Wednesday January 28, 1998
to Mark
yes I Do like Snow.
Yes I Do like snow people.
No. I never went down a big hill.
wht are birthday my birthday
is FEBRUARY twenty and you like
MIGHTY DUCKS. and you like
RAPTORS. I lost it is four to three
hcok.

Good Day Matthew

How have you been doing? The weather has been sooo beautiful lately, I have gotten to go roller blading for a few days. Do you Rollerblade? What do you like to do in the summer? I would like to thank you for inviting me to this Pen-Pal Day. I can't wait for it. I hope we have lots of fun.
See you soon; Mark

P.S. Easter's in a month, lots o' chocolate and lots o' Fun!

Matthew wrote his response letter without any assistance — a feat worth celebrating! He not only wrote independently, he decided to write the rough draft at his desk, leaving the safety of close proximity that he had with the group at the round table.

Matthew composed this letter on his own. The writing is very close to the way that Matthew actually spoke.

Wednesday, March 4, 1998

Dear Mark

I have been doing good. Yes I Rollerblade. In the summer I play Rollerblade hockey out side. How many goals have you got in hockey? I got 4 goals. Did you get body checked? I got body checked two times. I got hurt with two minutes left in the game. Do you like winter? Thank you for coming to our school.

From Matthew

Wednesday, March 4, 1998.
Der Marke
I have been doing
yes I Rollerblade
in the Summer I Play
Rollerblade hcokey out
S/D. how mne score
you got I got
4 gos? and you got Boek
check I got Boek

Check Too Tim and I
I wnt home in 2:00
in the game and
you like winter
and thenak you come

Penpal Day at the school occurred before Matthew responded to Mark's previous letter. On Penpal Day, Mark and Matthew spent almost two hours together, playing games, eating, and talking. From Matthew's letter, it seems they talked a lot about sports, and made an even stronger affective connection.

Matthew managed to answer all of Mark's questions and to ask three questions himself. His writing is vibrant and he takes risks, giving Mark more news/information than in any of his previous letters. We can now hear Matthew's voice in his writing. Hockey is his topic: He knows about hockey, and he knows he can share his love for hockey with Mark. He risks using the phrase "body check" — the big event he wanted to share with Mark.

In his original draft, Matthew uses very little punctuation, and the question mark he does use, is used incorrectly. However, the composition itself is very strong, and Matthew's spelling continues to develop, with transitional phonetic awareness apparent in words that are unfamiliar to him in written form. For the first time, Matthew remembered to add a closing to the letter. The rough draft for this letter was harder to read than some of the previous ones, but Matthew did not orally rehearse or revise it with someone else before scribing it on paper.

This is the "last letter" from Mark.

March 19/98

Dear Matthew

Wow, this is our last letter and all I can say is wow! I had so much fun this year. Thank you for having me to you school, and I hope you had Fun when you were at my school. I look at your letters and I can see a really good improvement. And now that your [sic] word processing I'm sure you can only improve more. Thank you for all the fun.

Mark

P.S. Have a Great Summer

Mark's letter is full of enthusiasm for Matthew and for their relationship. This last letter from Mark had four round stickers on it, each with a single superlative (GREAT ... SUPER ... WOW ... BRAVO) and lightning around each word. These reinforced both the relationship and Matthew's legitimacy as a writer. The praise from Mark about his improvement was particularly meaningful to Matthew.

Matthew's increased participation in the letter writing is especially evident in his last letter. Despite Matthew's great challenges in reading and writing, Mark and Matthew corresponded as two people interested in sharing their passion for sports and in finding other common interests.

Wednesday, April 1, 1998

Dear Mark,

This summer I am going to play rollerblade hockey. Do you have any fish? I have three fish. Do you like school? I do. Do you like Tye Dommi? I do because he scored five goals. In the summer we are going to the zoo. Do you have the video Kindergarten Cop? I do. I like it. Do you like Fall? I do. From Matthew

Matthew understands that Mark will not be writing to him and he extends the dialogue by actually answering the questions that he asks Mark. In this way, he both asks questions, as has been the protocol, and answers them, which is part of the dialogic nature of letter writing. That, in itself, is a very sophisticated response to what is the last letter of this long relationship.

Over the year Matthew became a much more confident writer. As the year progressed, with teacher support, shared interests with his penpal, and strong affective responses and encouragement from his penpal, the writing task gradually became less onerous for Matthew. He gained independence, further developed his reading and writing abilities, and used language for a very meaningful purpose: to build friendship.

• *Children Who Are Learning English as an Additional Language*

One of the most frequently asked questions of this program is "Can it be used with students who are learning English as an additional language?" Our response is a definitive, "Yes!" This penpal letter writing program can modified and individualized to meet the needs of all students, including those who are learning English as an additional language. The strategies suggested for children with special needs are directly applicable to children whose English is not proficient; and, as long as there is someone who can help interpret when necessary, these strategies are even appropriate for a child with little or no English at all.

Once the first couple of letters have been written, the predictable nature of the letter genre supports children who are learning English and enables them to take language risks.

DUOC: A PROFILE OF A CHILD LEARNING ENGLISH AS AN ADDITIONAL LANGUAGE

When Duoc (pronounced "Duke") came to Canada early in the new year from Vietnam, he spoke no English. Duoc's grade one teacher at the time focused on developing his oral language. He also received individual ESL assistance for one hour per week. At the end of the school year, it was decided that Duoc would remain in grade one the following September to carry on with the grade one program.

That September, it was quite evident that Duoc's oral language skills had grown considerably. His reading and writing skills, though, were just beginning to develop, so those skills would be the focus for the year. In reading, Duoc began to increase his sight word vocabulary and, before too long, he was able to read many predictable primer type books from the classroom library.

Written language was a real struggle for Duoc. Although he could scribe most letters of the alphabet, he would often write exactly the same, or very similar, few simple sentences every day to accompany the picture that he had made. Gently, he was given other story ideas, trying to ensure that he became familiar and comfortable with the whole process of writing before the expectations for him were increased. After about a month, Duoc did not appear to be making any progress. Around the same time, the penpal writing program was getting under way. This different approach to writing, with its strong scaffolding structures and predictive patterns, might help him go beyond his present restricted level of risk taking.

In our program, we particularly try to match children who are learning English as a second or additional language with someone of similar heritage, or as similar as possible. There was no one in the older penpal group of Vietnamese background; however, Duoc was ultimately matched with Hiren (pronounced "Heeren"), a first year teacher candidate of South Asian (Indian) Canadian heritage.

Hiren's first letter to Duoc was well above Duoc's reading level. It didn't matter because the letter was shared out loud with the class. Hiren's letter was still appealing, and things such as the exciting stationary invited Duoc into the penpal relationship.

Hiren's explicit reference to the fact that some people find his name difficult to pronounce establishes an immediate link between the two penpals. Hiren uses this shared concern to ask how to pronounce Duoc's name — without making Duoc feel different.

Duoc's first letter was an oral response to Hiren's letter, which he formulated with the assistance of his teacher. The standard sharing and re-reading had been completed. Features at the beginning of a letter (the date and the greeting) were discussed, then scribed for him. For Duoc, this was done in large primary sized letters, leaving lots of space directly below where Duoc could copy the letters underneath each word.

With assistance, Duoc located Hiren's questions, which were read to him. Again, with assistance, Duoc formulated some answers. Oftentimes, Duoc's one- or two-word answers needed to be elaborated to make complete sentences. This was done orally. Duoc was asked questions and through modeling, he elaborated and re-phrased the words into a complete sentence. He also looked back at Hiren's letter. Accordingly, Duoc also had to ask some questions. The letter was read again in a shared reading in which Duoc always took as much leadership as possible. After Duoc chose the closing, the entire letter was re-read again. When Duoc was satisfied with the final product, he underwrote the entire letter.

When Duoc was finished printing the letter, he and his teacher read the letter together once more. This process took several writing sessions to complete. When the letter was finished, Duoc drew a picture (which later had a sentence added to it). Duoc then decorated a large envelope in which the letter and picture were sent.

Hiren's second letter was written after the first Penpal Day. The meeting enabled Hiren to understand Duoc's language needs. Hiren's second letter was much shorter and was printed in a much larger size than the first letter had been.

The larger print was much more appropriate for Duoc. Hiren ensures strong affective messages by drawing pictures of the two penpals. As well, Hiren drew himself wearing traditional Indian clothing. These pictures and Hiren's reference to liking spicy food continue to affirm the similarities between the two penpals.

109

Duoc had not yet received Hiren's second letter and had to use Hiren's first letter as a model. This also meant that Duoc did not have new questions to respond to. Duoc was encouraged to write about the recent Penpal Day instead. This information was collaboratively composed and scribed for Duoc, in the same manner as the first letter. The questions Duoc asks were collaboratively formulated, and a closing was composed. The letter was scribed and Duoc underwrote it as he had the first.

Dear Hiren;

Hi I liked the at Trent. It

You could jump

liked the li

I play with Lego at school. I am 7. How old are you? Do you have a sister?

From Duoc

Duoc's third letter responds to Hiren's second letter. Duoc's letter was considerably longer, and he seemed to be more involved in the task. Duoc was becoming more familiar and comfortable with the letter writing activity and had also recently met Hiren at the Penpal Day.

Duoc answers Hiren's question about Halloween and offers a lot of new information about himself. With assistance, Duoc generated some questions to ask Hiren. Each letter subtly reinforces Duoc's oral, reading, and writing abilities.

This is Duoc's third letter.

Dear Hiren;
Dear Hiren;
Yes I went out
Yes I went out
for Halloween. I was
for Halloween. I was
a clown. My face
a clown. My face
was white and my
was white and my
eyes were blue
eyes were blue

...nd my nose was
nd my nose was
At school I
At school I
BINGO I like
BINGO I like
I like to play
I like to play
We have 2
we have 2
guys red and blue.
guys red and blue.

I like the computer.
I like the computer.
I do printing on
I do printing on
it. I had fun at
it. I had fun at
Trent. I liked to
Trent. I liked to
go with you. At
go with you. At
school ... in
school

the sand. At home
the sand. At home
play water gun 200
play water gun 200
my brother. How
my brother. How
our school? Where
our school? Where
you going for
you going for
have
have

a big chocolate
a big chocolate
bar from Trick or
bar from Trick or
Treating;
Treating;

From Duoc
From Duoc

In early December, Hiren had not yet written back to Duoc by the time he was to write a response letter. However, Duoc was still highly motivated and even generated the first sentence of the letter independently. This was Duoc's first attempt at writing his own letter. Without a letter to respond to, Duoc was encouraged to tell or ask Hiren about winter or Christmas. Although he needed a lot of assistance, he composed and scribed the letter by himself.

This is the rough draft of the first letter that Duoc composed and scribed himself.

DU·YoU HSeaCHetRee

MPlay show
RAB ; ToY

~~MA~~

I WTa ToYfoRCHe

This is the edited final copy of the first letter that Duoc composed and scribed himself.

Dear Hiren
Dear Hiren;

Do you have a
Do you have a

Christmas tree? I
Christmas tree? I

like playing in the
like playing in The

snow. I want a
Snow. I want a

y rabbit for
y rabbit for

ristmas.
istmas.

From Duoc
From Duoc

Hiren completed his third letter before the December holiday. However, Duoc did not receive it until after the holiday. Although this letter is late, Hiren still offers positive interaction with Duoc. He talks about how his family does not celebrate Christmas — something that sets his family apart from the majority of people in Canada.

Hiren's picture of the two penpals playing in the snow together is one way he shows Duoc that he cares about and enjoys their relationship.

Dear Duoc,

Do you see all the snow outside? Wow! There is so much Did you go outside and play? Did you make a snowman? I played in the snow too!!

I think that you are a great artist, Duoc. I love the way you draw apples, trees, and butterflies. Could you draw me a picture of a snowman?

Does your family celebrate Christmas? My older brother, mother and father really don't, but we still buy gifts and visit friends.

Well, I hope you enjoy your holidays. Have a happy new year!!

Your Penpal, HIREN

It is now Hiren's turn to respond to Duoc without a letter to reply to. Hiren refers to a singing angel that Duoc had made for him. He also enclosed a toy truck with the letter (which is penpal contraband). More importantly, there is also a picture of a bunny with a basket of apples to illustrate a verse. Duoc really loved this picture! It was very well done, and it was tangible evidence that Hiren listens and responds to what Duoc says in his letters in a unique and creative way. With the picture, Hiren is incorporating the fact that Duoc likes apples and rabbits — information that Duoc had shared with him in previous letters. Duoc wrote the response to this letter all by himself.

Dear Duoc,

Hello! I am sorry for not writing to you sooner. Remember Duoc, we are still **pals**!

Thank you very much for the singing angel you made for me. I think that you are very talented.

We did not have a Christmas tree, but I got a jean jacket! It keeps me warm when I play in the snow.

In your letter you told me you wanted a rabbit. I did not buy one, but I drew a picture of a rabbit for you

The rabbit's name is
Muddy Bunny. I hope you
like it.
I am also sending you
a little toy truck.
HAVE FUN!
Your Friend,
Hiren.

Muddy Bunny
Carrots are yummy!
Carrots are fantastic!
But Duoc likes apple
So I bought him
A basket !!!

This letter showed quite a strong progression for Duoc in the degree of independence in writing the letter. Although he is still not separating words very well, in the first sentence, spaces are beginning to make their appearance. Underwriting is still an important bridge for Duoc as he continues to gain independence and a conceptual understanding of individual words when he writes.

Thank you for the toy truck.
Thank you for the picture of the
rabbit. How are you doing?
Do you go skating?

ThankYou for The toy truck Duoc
Thank you for the reofdroidb it for you
picty
Howhyoudoing?
Do GoSkol+e

Duoc writes his next letter without assistance. Penpal Day at the school occurred in between Hiren's last letter and this one, so the two had been in physical contact recently. Also, Hiren gave Duoc a birthday card at Penpal Day. So, even though Duoc had not received a letter from Hiren, there were important topics he could write about.

Dear Hiren,

Thank you for coming to Penpal day. Thank you for the birthday card that you gave to me. I was sick with a cold. Please come to my school.

From, Duoc.

He now includes the salutation as part of his letter. The letter length and spelling accuracy have increased. Duoc is using more complete thoughts and full sentences. A model letter would be scribed for him, but he would not underwrite it this time. He would use the letter as a model, scribing it on a separate sheet of paper himself.

Duoc's final class letter to Hiren was sent in mid-April. He had not heard from Hiren in some time. Duoc wondered why he was not receiving any letters from Hiren, and he was allowed to write to Hiren about this. (As sometimes happens, a letter from Hiren arrived the day after Duoc's letter was sent. Enclosed with the letter were photographs from the school Penpal Day.)

Dear Hiren,

Why do you not write to me? I go to school to learn English. I made a kangaroo for Miss Gall. I got a needle from the doctor. Please come visit me. Will you keep writing to me?

From, Duoc.

Hiren's letter indicates that he will continue writing to Duoc even though the Penpal Program is officially over. As well, he draws another picture for Duoc with the bunny/apples theme and also includes a rhyme.

Dear Duoc

Hi buddy! I didn't write to you for a few weeks because I was waiting for the pictures! Do you like them? I do. I think you have a nice smile. I had a lot of fun with you Duoc. I'm going to

visit you soon! I had fun writing to you. I will still write to you until the end of June. Would you like that? Thank-you for the pictures Duoc. You draw wonderful bunnies! I also think you are a good friend. Bye Duoc, and see you soon.

YOUR FRIEND,
Hiren

Duoc and his friend, the Bunny, are having fun, eating apples and reading in the sun!

In May, Hiren sends Duoc a letter after he has returned home from university. He emphasizes his ongoing friendship with Duoc, and includes a book that he promises to read with Duoc the following year. (In fact, he did volunteer to be Duoc's penpal for a second year — and even a third year after that.)

(1)

Dear Duoc,

Hello there! How are you? I moved back to Toronto for the summer. Toronto is where my real home is. I have been busy for the past two weeks spending time with my family, and all of my old friends! But I have not forgotten about you Duoc — my new friend !!!

(2)

I am glad that I met you Duoc. You are a fun person to be with. Everyone in Mrs. Gall's class likes you. You are a talented artist, and your reading, and writing has improved a lot during the year. Good for you Duoc!

Play outside during the summer and have fun, but keep reading! I am sending you a book. You will find it

(3)

to read so get someone to read to you. Next year, we will read a book together!

Thank-you for all the pictures and stickers (and book!)

Write me a letter soon so I can write to you once more before school is over.

Bye!

Your friend,
Hiren

Duoc's final letter of the year, like Hiren's letter, is not written as a letter that is ending a relationship. At this time, all regular penpal program activities had ceased, so it was quite special for Duoc to receive a letter and a book from Hiren.

Duoc's letter (translated) in response to Hiren's indication of ongoing friendship.

Dear Hiren,

I want to thank you for the book. You are the best penpal. Tomorrow I have card club. We trade cards in card club. Lisa is going to help me with my work. I like the pictures that you made for me.

From Duoc.

Duoc's final two letters show dramatic growth in terms of his writing abilities. More growth was noted in Duoc's letter writing than in the regular story writing sessions, where children drew a picture and then wrote a story about what is going on in the picture.

Hiren was not the most punctual writer, sometimes missing deadlines and, thus, leaving Duoc without a model to work from. However, when Hiren did write, he did so with creativity and genuine interest in Duoc. So, despite irregular delivery, the letters showed consistent caring when they did arrive, which enabled Duoc to respond positively and to develop his writing skills.

Duoc's letter writing skills developed in response to a purposeful writing activity. His audience was real and alive, and responded to him as a person of value. The concrete structures and models of the penpal program gave Duoc the framework to help him get started. The photographs taken of the two penpals at the first Penpal Day, the creativity of Hiren's letters, and the strong support for Duoc provided motivation. In addition to the larger language arts program and day-to-day life experiences, the language skills Duoc gained from this letter writing relationship helped him become a more independent writer.

Based on the positive results with Duoc in less than ideal circumstances, it is possible to see how a similar letter writing program would be beneficial to any ESL student who is an emergent writer. Although Duoc initially required more time (assistance and encouragement) than the average student, the program in general did not have to be modified in extraordinary ways to ensure his success in the activity. The accumulation of letters in his penpal folder — both his own and Hiren's — was testimony to his increasing abilities in written language.

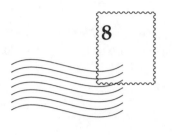

Using Penpal Letters
to Assess Language Arts

In Chapter 8, we consider ways to include penpal letters as part of ongoing assessment of language development. We see the penpal activities as one part of a larger range of activities and tasks, but we feel they are an important part of our language development assessment strategies. The penpal program provides opportunities for children to demonstrate what they have learned in a real life situation. In this context, teachers use teaching/learning strategies that incorporate both whole language and discrete teaching of language conventions. Thus, it is common for a teacher to give a short lesson on phonics, for instance, with children engaged in activities long associated with that kind of learning. However, in the same classroom, the children may also be reading trade books, writing journal responses, and creating their own stories based on a book that they shared as a whole class. We make the assumption that many of these types of language activities occur in most classrooms, enabling the teacher to refer to language awareness knowledge (such as phonics or punctuation conventions) with children as they are writing.

It is now common practice in most English-speaking countries to assess reading and writing across a diverse range of language activities and tasks. Narrative/story writing has long been a common task in primary language arts curriculum; however, recent curriculum and assessment documents also emphasize the importance of report writing, letter writing, and descriptive writing. We read many curriculum documents in order to develop our penpal program. We have synthesized information from several curriculum documents, such as the U.S. Assessing

Student Performance Grades K–5 (National Council of Teachers of English, 1997); the Canadian Ontario Curriculum Exemplars Grades 1–8: Writing (Ontario Ministry of Education, 1999); and the National Curriculum for England 2000 (Qualifications and Curriculum Authority, 2000), in order to develop a penpal program that supports and enhances any language arts curriculum.

Penpal letter writing and reading provide an insightful snapshot of certain kinds of language development. For most children, the penpal activities are powerful because they are meaningful. The child is motivated to communicate with a significant "other" and in a literal sense they must learn and strengthen their language skills to do so. Much of the learning is reinforced almost every month when the children replicate the same tasks — reading and writing a friendly letter. The focus on genre means that the wider activities around the task remain very constant. The similarity and consistency of the activities from month to month make certain kinds of development more noticeable in assessment.

There are multiple ways of assessing language development and achievement. We use terminology from various language arts frameworks. Our intention is to give teachers support in assessment for various purposes, while recognizing that children must be seen as human beings involved in sociocultural contexts — and the real goal is to help children understand and use language in meaningful ways. In this chapter, we provide assessment tools that you can use directly or modify to suit your own purposes.

It is important to identify the language arts strengths of a child and to work from those strengths. That is why putting the date on each letter is so critical: It will help you track the achievement demonstrated by a child at a particular point in time. It is also important to know how much and what kind of assistance a child needs or uses to write their letters. In doing this, you can discover which skills and tasks need work and which things the children do independently. We encourage children who need assistance to use it; but, equally, we celebrate the children's increasing independence as they become able and confident enough to write letters on their own. All of these elements provide important information about the child — both for reporting purposes and for indicating future teaching/learning directions.

Self-assessment components in the wider assessment can be valuable tools. Proponents of authentic assessment see self-assessment as one of the most important aspects of the assessment strategy. You will find some tools for self-assessment in the latter part of this chapter.

Important Aspects of Teacher Assessment in Penpal Letter Writing

- *Identify the child's strengths.*
  - What skills and knowledge can they already demonstrate?
  - Is there evidence of emergent new ability?

- *Ensure that every letter is dated.*
  - Observe a child's development over specific time periods.

- *Keep photocopies of the children's draft letters and the final version. Keep dated copies of the older penpals' letters, too.*
  - Determine how reliant the child is on those drafts and letters.
  - Carefully track specific aspects of development.

- *Write anecdotal notes.*
  - Identify the child's use of assistance and describe the child's motivation/initiative in completing writing and reading tasks.

The Language Arts Curriculum — At the Heart of Assessment

Virtually every curriculum document that was written in recent years was written in terms of outcomes-based/expectations-based learning. Assessment, therefore, focuses on the child's actual and demonstrated understandings and abilities. A child might not fulfill a given expectation in one teaching/learning activity; however, over a period of time in which the child has opportunities to learn, practice, and master the skill or knowledge, you can observe the child's ongoing progress and achievement. Accurate assessment in an outcomes-based/expectations-based curriculum depends on opportunities for the children to demonstrate ongoing learning.

The first step is to familiarize yourself with the expectations/outcomes in the curriculum developed for your particular school-area and the age-group you teach. When you focus on these expectations, it is easier to build your assessment around the activities that will help the children achieve them.

Most programs for early reader/writers include expectations associated with conventions: forming letters; leaving spaces between words; using periods; writing in complete sentences; using phonics to spell words; and adding to sight vocabulary. As well, most language arts programs for the age-group focus on reading/writing for meaning; developing ideas in writing; understanding context (and responding accordingly); and understanding how to use language to communicate meaningfully in a variety of settings.

Children participating in the program have several opportunities in each letter-writing cycle to listen, read, ask and answer questions, consider context, and write (usually in response to other written communication). The penpal program thus offers several opportunities and ways for you to assess a child's progress.

Each penpal exchange allows you to monitor the children's accomplishments. When you assess any response letter, note the meaning that the child is communicating and the extent to which the child is developing ideas. It can be easy to underestimate (or grossly overestimate) a child's abilities. The degree of meaning-making, reasoning, and communication is only fully understood when you know what the older penpal wrote (context); what support structures in the penpal's letter are available to the child; and what other assistance the child received. These are very helpful considerations in assessing just what an emerging writer can accomplish and with what degree of independence. That assessment is necessary in order for you to focus the child on the learning priorities for the next letter. Without your professional guidance, the children can be overwhelmed by the number and variety of expectations.

Penpal Letter Assessment Framework

Independence
- What degree of assistance does the child need in order to perform the task at the level demonstrated?

Conventions of Language
- Letter formation
- Use of spacing
- Language awareness exhibited through
  - Spelling development, including use of spelling resources
  - Conventional use of grammar
  - Conventional use of punctuation

Reasoning
- Responding to questions and information in their penpal's letter
- Complexity of thinking exhibited through content and sentence structure
- Expression of personal point of view
- Ability to relate personal life experiences to the topics at hand

Organization of Ideas
- Beginning, middle, and end to the writing
- Structure of writing
- Internal linkage of ideas
- Use of paragraphing

Communication
- Audience awareness (need for complete sentences, referents, additional detail)
- Inclusion of details to support ideas
- Voice
- Vocabulary

Language Arts Curriculum Frameworks

When we were writing this book, we analyzed the language arts curriculum from several regions, including western and central Canada, the United Kingdom, and the United States. We learned that the organizational frameworks for language arts are all looking for similar features of development and achievement. Although most of the elements of reading and writing are the same in these frameworks, they may fall into different categories for assessment.

The assessment framework provided in this book is our interpretation of the standard expectations found in a solid language arts curriculum. The framework identifies the following features of development: Independence; Conventions of Language; Reasoning; Organization of Ideas; and Communication.

Assessing Early Reader/Writers in the Penpal Program

A CASE STUDY: ERIC

Jamie, the older penpal, prints in large, very readable font in her first letter to Eric. She leaves a good amount of space between each word and writes a standard opening letter, two pages long. In his response, Eric writes more than a full page.

Dear Eric,

I hope you had a good Thanksgiving. Did you have turkey? Halloween is coming soon. What are you going t[...] for Halloween? I have a d[...] name is Case. Do you have[...] All the leaves on the tre[...]

changing colors. My favorite color of the leaves is red. [Written in red marker.] What is your favorite color? Please write back.

From
Jamie

This short draft is Eric's first letter to Jamie.

Independence

Eric was unable to complete this task without significant assistance. Nevertheless, the amount of text scripted is impressive, given his skill level. At this point, Eric has met Jamie at the Penpal Day. The difference between this letter and his first letter is significant.

Wednesday November 12, 1997

Dear Jamie,

How are you? Are you excited for our next Penpal Day? I did have Thanksgiving. Yes, I have a dog. My favorite color of leaf is brown. When is your birthday? Did you dress up on Halloween? What is your favorite season?

See you later,

from Eric.

In the first letter, Eric scripts only the date and salutation. The fact that he scripts so much text in this letter shows a remarkable difference in his initiative and motivation.

Conventions of Language

Eric uses left-right progression in his writing. Although his letter formation is inconsistent, his letters are, for the most part, decipherable. He often includes only initial and final consonants when spelling independently (e.g., "WN" for "when;" "DRS" for "dress"). Eric can usually copy the correct spelling of a word when it is shown to him. He is beginning to include spaces between his words, a factor that helps immensely in decoding his writing.

Reasoning

With teacher support, Eric answers the questions that Jamie asks him, and in the order that the questions are asked. Thus, both the teacher and the penpal letter provide reasoning and organizational support for Eric.

The question–answer format prescribed in the program is a scaffold that ensures some variation in sentence structure. It seems doubtful that at this time Eric would initiate different sentence structures were it not for the assistance he receives.

Organization of Ideas
Eric follows penpal letter protocol in his opening but, after that, the organization is somewhat list-like as he answers the questions Jamie asks.

Communication
Eric provides only minimal information when he answers Jamie's questions. He is not following the pattern that Jamie establishes when she writes about her pet dog and tells Eric its name.

Commentary
There is much that Eric is unable to demonstrate yet. However, given the obvious difficulty of this task for him, the amount of text he generates remains noteworthy and worth celebrating. This significant amount of text, in itself, demonstrates how meaningful this writing task is for him, and confirms his view of himself as a penpal writer.

Assessing Transitional Reader/Writers in the Penpal Program

A CASE STUDY: GREG

In this exchange between Sam and Greg, we see Greg's appropriation of Sam's opening, including her use of an exclamation point. This kind of direct appropriation is not uncommon and often extends to just a very slight re-wording of an older penpal's question. We do support this kind of scaffolding but, again, keep the older penpal's letter at hand when you are doing your assessment.

October 16, 1999

Hi Greg!

I had a great summer. I drove through 4 different provinces when I moved from Alberta to Ontario. Trent University is awesome! I have a lot of friends and great teachers. The trees at the University are very pretty right now because of all the fall colors. I have also seen the movie "A Bug's Life." My favorite characters are the potato bugs because they are so silly and make

laugh. What other movies do like? When you write me please me how Trick or Treating went. ou get a lot of candy? I bet one will like your Grim Reaper me. It sounds very cool. I vait until your next letter.

riend,

t a picture of myself on I am sending with this

Wednesday, October 27, 1999

Hi Sam!

I like Scream the movie. Do you like any more movies? I didn't go trick or treating yet. Do you like Scream the movie? What did you do on Reading Break? Are you going out for Halloween?

All the best,

Greg

Independence
Greg is on task very quickly and writes this letter independently, using Sam's letter as a model. He also uses a topic idea brainstormed orally by the class beforehand (i.e., asking your penpal what they did on the university reading break).

Conventions
Greg forms letters correctly and uses upper and lower case letters appropriately. His sense of punctuation is developing well, and although he uses commas instead of periods at the ends of sentences, he does recognize the sentence unit. Question marks are used correctly. Monosyllabic words are spelled correctly or phonetically plausibly, showing Greg's awareness of spelling conventions, such as the double "e" in "screem" and "reeding." His use of the double "n" in "enny" and the double "r" in "morre" show his incomplete but growing awareness of double consonant conventions.

Reasoning
The movie topic is somewhat developed, although Greg does not pick up Sam's technique of talking about a favorite part of the movie or providing detail about why he likes it.

Organization of Ideas
The letter has a strong sense of beginning, middle, and end. Greg goes beyond the rote performance of class routines in his use of Sam's salutation and in his appropriation of the closing, "All the best." It is likely a closing that he heard from someone else's penpal letter during sharing time.

Communication
Greg's voice is quite strong and, although the vocabulary is somewhat limited, sentence structure has some variation.

Commentary

At this stage of the writing relationship, the penpals are still getting to know one another. Greg has sensed from Sam's letter that "movies" are a good topic, and his question about her university reading break shows his ability to adopt Sam's perspective to a limited degree at least.

Assessing Fluent Reader/Writers in the Penpal Program

A CASE STUDY: ANDREW

Andrew and Allyson met each other on Penpal Day and quickly established quite a strong bond.

October 16, 1999

Dear Andrew A.,

I had a fun time with you on penpal day. Thank you very m for coming. I also had a gre Thanksgiving. I like going f Do you go fishing a lot in t summer? What is your fav sport? I like hockey. Do y a lot of hockey cards?

I am very busy at school because I have to read a lot. Do you like to read? I took your picture and hung it on my wall. You draw very well. I also liked

the envelope that you made. I hope you are having a good time at school. The picture I sent you is of me during the first week of school, before I cut my hair. I will write again soon. Bye.

Your Friend,

Allyson

Wednesday, October 27,1999

Dear Allyson,

I had a fun time on Penpal day too. I am glad I could come. I do go fishing a lot in the summer. My favorite spot for fishing is the Otonabee River. Are you going to have a Halloween party at Trent? How is it going at Trent?

From, Andrew A.

Dear Allyson, Wednesday, October 27, 1999

I had a fun on Penpal day to. I am glad I cood come. I do go fishing a lot in the summer. MY favoriti SPat for fishing is the otonabe river. Are You going to have a hallaween party at trent? How is it going at trent?

from Andrew A.

Independence

Andrew shows great initiative and independence in writing his letter to Allyson. In many ways his enthusiasm and motivation are apparent even in the tone of his letter.

Conventions

Andrew has strong control over handwriting, with letters being clearly formed and consistent in height. His spelling demonstrates a strong control of monosyllabic spelling, of the suffix "-ing," and of spelling strategies for words he spells phonetically. He uses upper case letters correctly at the beginning of sentences and shows awareness of using them for proper nouns as well. All the sentences have appropriate end punctuation, and Andrew uses commas correctly in the date and salutation.

Reasoning

Andrew develops both of the main ideas in his letter by writing two sentences about each of them. The detail that he provides, such as noting his favorite fishing spot, greatly enhance the letter.

Organization of Ideas

Although Andrew does not use paragraphing techniques, his ideas are organized in paragraph-like ways, with main ideas and supporting detail or extension chunked together. He is ready to be taught the convention of paragraphing.

Communication

Andrew's voice is strong and his choice of vocabulary expresses his feelings clearly. His extension in the second line ("I am glad I could come.") reinforces his first sentence in a genuine way and sets the tone for the rest of the letter. Sentences are varied and begin to develop complexity.

Commentary

Andrew's letter reflects a maturity of thinking and feeling that goes beyond that of most of his peers. His letter conveys a deep connection between the two writers, with Andrew communicating about personally meaningful aspects of his life and relating those to what is meaningful to his audience.

Student Self-Assessment

Many agree that self-assessment is a very important learning activity, and having students assess their own work in our penpal program can be a very effective learning strategy. However, the degree of self-assessment and of editing the students can manage is closely related to each child's reading and writing fluency. Thus, for our earliest reader/writers, the task of writing the letter initially involves much harder work and longer time than it does for more fluent reader/writers. And, similarly, the amount of editing by the teacher is much greater.

In fact, our earliest readers may scribe just a bit of the letter themselves and then dictate the larger bulk. During any dictation, it is appropriate for the person scribing to ask the child whether or not something sounds right; whether it says what the author really wants it to say; whether it gives enough detail. For these children, the next part of the writing task then involves copying the final version of the letter, oftentimes writing on top of the teacher's printing or writing underneath it.

However, more able reader/writers should be editing their own letter before they take their work to the teacher. The template, Editing My Work, can be used for many different writing tasks, including that of penpal letter writing.

Similarly, children should be thinking about the quality of the work they did: They should be able to identify the things they have done well and the things they need to work on. Even early reader/writers can begin to use this form of self-assessment. (See Thinking About My Work, page 132.)

Rubrics of Levels of Achievement

Many jurisdictions are using rubrics of levels of achievement to assess student performance. Although specifics of the rubric structure may vary, the kinds of development being reviewed for assessment remain consistent. The following rubric for a friendly letter may be helpful, although its structure for the standards of achievement may differ slightly from your own. The same categories of assessment are used in this rubric as were used in the assessment of letters earlier in this chapter.

Rubric of Levels of Achievement in Letter Writing: Grades 1 and 2

Category	Level 1	Level 2	Level 3	Level 4
	Achievement falls below the standard	**Achievement approaches the standard**	**Achievement meets the standard**	**Achievement exceeds the standard**
Independence • Ability to perform task independently	• Is unable to complete tasks independently; requires significant assistance	• Completes tasks with some independence but still requires some assistance	• Completes tasks with significant independence; is usually self-directed	• Completes tasks independently; is self-directed
• Responsibility	• Avoids responsibility for completing the writing tasks on time and with care	• Sometimes accepts responsibility for completing writing tasks on time and with care	• Regularly accepts responsibility for completing writing tasks on time and with care	• Always accepts responsibility for completing writing tasks on time and with care
Conventions of Language • Spelling, grammar, punctuation	• Application of written conventions is minimal (e.g., sound-letter correspondence is not evident; words are not divided by spaces)	• Application of written conventions is incomplete and inconsistent in relation to grade level expectations of phonemic awareness and punctuation	• Control of written conventions is sound in relation to early phonemic awareness; correctly spells vocabulary appropriate for grade level; generally accurate use of punctuation expected grade level (Gr. 1: period at the end of a sentence; comma after the salutation. Gr. 2: question mark)	• Application of written conventions includes attempts at polysyllabic words and vowel combinations; awareness and some use of punctuation beyond that expected at grade level (e.g., Gr. 1: question mark; Gr. 2: apostrophe)
	• Printing is not legible	• Printing is inconsistent re. letter formation	• Letters are accurately formed and consistent in size	• Letters are accurately formed and consistent in size
	• Errors interfere with decoding	• Errors interfere with decoding	• Errors do not interfere with decoding	• Errors seem to be the result of risks taken by the writer

Category	Level 1 Achievement falls below the standard	Level 2 Achievement approaches the standard	Level 3 Achievement meets the standard	Level 4 Achievement exceeds the standard
Reasoning • Responding to penpal letter	• Makes little reference to the questions or information in their penpal's letter	• Makes simple reference to the questions and information in their penpal's letter and with assistance generates new questions	• Responds completely to the questions and information in their penpal's letter; and generates new questions with occasional assistance	• Responds with detail to the questions and information in their penpal's letter; may extend the question with new information; generates new questions with minimal assistance
• Making connections	• Rarely makes connections to personal life experiences	• Makes simple or few connections to personal life experiences	• Makes appropriate but limited connections to personal experiences	• Extends dialogue with connections to personal life experiences
Organization of Ideas • Letter format	• Control of letter format is not evident	• Control of letter format is evident but inconsistent or incomplete	• Consistent control of letter format	• Uses varieties of format (e.g., closings)
• Flow	• Sequence of ideas is not evident	• Sequence of ideas is interrupted	• Sequence of ideas is logical	• May extend ideas over several letters
Communication • Audience awareness	• Little awareness of the audience (older penpal)	• Beginning awareness of the audience (older penpal)	• Communicates directly with the older penpal	• Effective and engaging communication with older penpal
• Vocabulary	• Vocabulary remains extremely limited	• Simple, familiar use of vocabulary	• Effective use of vocabulary, including some found in the older penpal's letter	• Takes risks with new vocabulary
• Voice	• Personal voice is not evident	• Mechanical voice that may directly mimic the penpal	• Personal voice begins to emerge	• Distinct and confident use of personal voice
Comments:				

Name _____ Date _____

Editing My Work

What I did to edit my writing

- **I checked the meaning of my writing:**

    Does it make sense?

    Did I leave out any important information or words?

    Have I included enough detail?

- **I checked my capitals (upper case letters):**
    - at the beginning of sentences
    - on names
    - on dates

- **I checked my punctuation:**
    - periods   .
    - question marks   ?
    - quotation marks   ""
    - exclamation marks   !

- **I checked my spelling:**
    - in my personal word book
    - on class word lists
    - in a dictionary

- **I checked my sentences for:**
    - better words
    - missing words
    - extra words

Name: _____   Date: _____

Thinking About My Work

Title of Work: _____

☆　☆　☆　☆

• I have circled the star that shows how well I did.

• This is what I did really well!

I _____

_____

_____

• This is what I need to work on.

I need to _____

_____

_____

_____

E-Mail Keypals — The Practicalities

9

The penpal program presented in the previous chapters of this book was premised on children handwriting their letters to their older penpals — which is not to say that e-mail keypals will not work. Every type of communication has its own advantages and disadvantages, and electronic communication affords some interesting possibilities.

Penpals or Keypals?

There is no right or wrong choice. It comes down to knowing about your children, their access and ability to use the technology, and the purpose of the reading and writing they will do.

We found that using handwritten letters has an advantage that is most evident in assessment. The children's handwritten first drafts provide an extraordinary amount of information about their cognitive-kinesthetic ability to form letters, their phonemic awareness, their awareness of conventions of spelling and punctuation, and their communication skills when they incorporate drawings and illustrations in the text of the letter. For our emergent and early writers, this information is essential for the kinds of one-on-one, informal assessment and teaching that are a regular part of the teaching/learning process.

One of our biggest concerns about using e-mail is that some computer programs make it impossible to see these kinds of information, for many computer programs automatically correct common spelling errors and automatically place upper case letters in words that follow certain punctuation, such as periods and colons.

We encourage our more able children to use the computer to key in their final drafts as an additional copy of their final letter. They add computer graphics as is appropriate. However, this "keying in" is not really electronic communication: It results in computer-generated print.

Exchanging letters by e-mail (keypals) provides the option of genuine electronic communication. Many of the university penpals have an e-mail address. (And that can be a big help for the coordinator, especially when emergencies or changes occur at either end. E-mail gives the coordinator much faster access to several penpals simultaneously.) A keypal program offers the advantage that children gain confidence and familiarity with the keyboard, the software, and the concept of electronic communication.

Keypal possibilities were a natural outgrowth in one classroom in our penpal program. With university students as the older penpals, our penpal program ends in April when their academic year ends. However, school for the children continues until the end of June. The writing relationship can be extended if both penpals have Internet access. In this classroom, the children had teacher-supervised Internet access at school, and some of the older penpals had Internet access from their homes.

This particular grade two class had become familiar with the Internet and e-mail that year. The teacher communicated via e-mail with the program coordinator about things such as Penpal Days and the topics the children were studying. Occasionally an e-mail would be sent to a specific penpal regarding any important information which that penpal needed to know (e.g., family separation). The whole class had also been communicating via e-mail with two teachers from the school who were on exchange in Australia. Those teachers periodically sent a class letter via e-mail. Some children whom the teachers had taught were encouraged to send a reply from home if they had Internet access.

Thus, when the penpal letter writing program was drawing to a close in April, the teacher suggested that interested students could ask their penpals if they would like to continue writing via e-mail until the end of June. The penpal program provided a context for continued communication, and e-mail was an appropriate medium because a local pick-up/drop-off point for letters would no longer be available. In addition, and perhaps more importantly, e-mail communication had already been modeled for the children, so they were familiar with the concept and the routines involved. Only two children in the class chose to become involved in the e-mail continuation of their penpal relationship. A third student began a correspondence with someone he didn't already know, but who shared his deep interest in baseball. The following section outlines the progress of those keypals.

A CASE STUDY: GREG AND SARAH

Greg and Sarah had established a penpal relationship during the year. They both used the familiar friendly letter format. Thus, the keypal procedures were built on a strong foundation of expectations and relationship. Sarah began the e-mail correspondence, and her letter arrived via the teacher's e-mail address and was printed out at school. Sarah's first e-mail included a smiley-face, :) , a common signifier in informal e-mail communication.

Greg was familiar with Write Along, an early word processing program for primary children, but he used Clarisworks when he composed his letters. Copying Greg's letter into e-mail was a problem, so the letter was re-typed directly online, while Greg watched and collaboratively made changes. This process was time consuming and complicated. Greg's biggest struggle was learning the more sophisticated word processing in Clarisworks.

Greg's draft letter, and the final copy that Sarah received by e-mail.

> Dear Sarah
>
> I am fine. I did not have a good Easter I got sick. Yes I did get some chocolate. I coloured three Easter eggs. Do you like the rain? I hope you do good on your tests. i like baby kittens their so cute. do you like the colour blue? do you like pizza? who is your friend at school? mine is Timothy. I got an adidas back pack. And an adidas coat. My brother got an adidas hat. I got a soccer ball for Easter. Do you like chocolate? I got a basketball. Do you have basketball? write to you   soon   your friend Greg

Greg's final copy.

> Printed by:
> Title: Re: Greg   Public School
>   Thursday, April 23, 1998 8:42:41 PM
>   Page 1 of 1
>   Tuesday, April 21, 1998 8:25:22 AM
>   Message
>
> **From:**   Molly F. Gall
> **Subject:**   Re: Greg
> **To:**   [Sarah]
>
> Dear Sarah
>
> I am fine. I did not have a good Easter. i got sick. yes I did get some chocolate. I coloured three Easter eggs. Do you like the rain? I hope you do good on your tests. i like baby kittens, they're so cute. Do you like the colour blue? Do you like pizza? Who is your friend at school? Mine is Timothy. I got an Adidas back pack and an Adidas coat. My brother got an Adidas hat.. I got a soccer ball for Easter. Do you like chocolate? I got a basketball. Do you have a basketball? Write to you soon, your friend Greg.

Greg's letter lacks paragraphing and some details are misplaced. Although it seems a bit disorganized, it contains information that furthers the dialogue through new topics. Sarah's response letter lacks paragraphing as well (possibly a common feature of informal e-mail letters), but the information in her letter is chunked in paragraph-like topics.

```
Printed by:                Public School
Title:                                          Wednesday, April 29, 1998  3:38:58 AM
                Tuesday, April 28, 1998 1:57:32 PM                        Page 1 of 1
                Message

From:
Subject:
To:
Attachments:           Internet Header                              1K
```

Dear Greg,

I am sorry to hear that you had a bad Easter! It is too bad that you got sick! I do like the rain. If it isn't cold out or thundering I sometimes even walk in the rain! I think that my tests went well. I am really glad that they are done! I am at home now. It is a nice change but soon I have to find a job! The colour blue is very nice. I have a lot of blue clothes. My friend as school is Melody. She is from Sarnia like I am so I have known her for a long time. Did I meet Timothy when I was at penpal day? I love pizza and chocolate! You picked two of my favourite foods to ask me about. I like pizza with pineapple! Do you like pineapple? It is nice that you got Adidas stuff! Guess what! My brother has an Adidas hat just like your brother! Neat! A basketball will be a fun thing to have in the summer! I like to play basketball sometimes but I am not very good at it and I am too short to do a slam dunk! How is school going? Are you doing anything fun and exciting in gym class? How are your brother and sister? Do you play on any sports teams in the summertime? Write back as soon as you can! It is fun to get email! Take care.

Your friend,

Sarah :)

When Sarah responds to Greg's questions, answering them seriously, she affirms Greg's legitimacy and maintains their connectedness. Her responses deepen the exchanges, and her tone is one of great fondness for Greg. This tone dominates the e-mail exchange over the next weeks.

The tonal effects of the older penpals' letters were often achieved and reinforced with color and illustration. It is important to recognize that tone can still be maintained via e-mail — through particular attention to the younger writer's topics, vocabulary choice, and use of exclamation points.

```
                                           Wednesday, May 13, 1998  8:47:44 AM
Printed by:            Public School                              Page 1 of 1
Title: Re: Greg
                Tuesday, May 12, 1998 11:52:04 AM
                Message

From:       [Sarah]
Subject:    Re: Greg
To:         Molly F. Gall                                   1K
Attachments:        Internet Header
```

May 12, 1998

Dear Greg,

Everything is going well here. How are you doing? I am trying to find a job for the summer. I still haven't had any luck. I wished my Dad 'happy birthday' for you and he says 'thank you'. I do like strawberries, peaches and apples. Apples are really good with peanut butter on them. What does your uncle do at Trent? Is he a teacher? How is the weather in Peterborough? Here it is cool and rainy. It is supposed to get warm by the weekend. I saw a fire yesterday when I was out driving. There were fire trucks and police cars all over the place. It was exciting. Why is March your favorite month? I hope that you are well. Write soon.

Your friend,

Sarah :)

Tuesday, May 26, 1998 11:49:53 AM
Message

From: [Sarah]
Subject: Re: Greg
To: Molly F. Gall
Attachments: Internet Header   1K

Hello Greg,

How are you? I am fine. What have you been up to in Peterborough? I have been trying to get a job. I finally got one! I am going to be working for the city, running activities for kids in the parks. It should be fun. Are you really busy in school right now? My brother is going on a class trip to Niagara Falls this week. He is very excited. Have you ever been to Niagara Falls? It is really neat! Have you been collecting Beanie Babies at McDonalds? I have collected four of them. They are really cute! I have the dog, the giraffe, the monkey, and the hippo! I can't wait to get the cat! Too bad that it isn't purple! I hope that you are well. Write soon.

Your friend,

Sarah :)

Sarah fills her letters with news and new topics of potential interest to Greg: Niagara Falls and Beanie Babies. Her specific details and voice show her enthusiasm for writing to Greg. In his response, Greg continues the dialogue, and the day-to-day life of this particular seven-year-old emerges quite strongly. The overall writing and reading that Greg had been doing throughout the year was very successful. In fact, the teacher adds a post script to one of Greg's e-mails, alluding to Greg's "surprise" for Sarah: a book that he has written and wants her to have. The two keypals continue writing, and the final correspondence of the school year shows the bond they established throughout the year.

Greg's draft and final copy.

Hello Sarah.

Iam fine I've been fishing and swiming for the last two weeks. I am not that busy at school. No I have not been to Niagara falls before. No I have not been collecting beanie babies at Mcdonalds.Iam glad to hear that you found a job! Iam excited about summer break. Do you like camping? I like camping. What is your address? I have a surprise for you.
Do you like cherrys? I like cherrys. write back soon.

Your pal Greg.

Tuesday, June 02, 1998 11:02:26 AM
Page 1 of 1

...ay May 29, 1998

Hello Sarah,

I am fine. I've been fishing and swimming for the last two weeks. I am not that busy at school. No I have not been to Niagara Falls before. No I have not been collecting Beanie Babies at MacDonald's . I am glad to hear that you found a job! I am excited about summer break. Do you like camping? What is your address? I have a surprise for you. Do you like cherries? I like cherries. Write back soon.

   Your pal Greg,

p.s. Sarah, Greg has written a book for you that we want to mail to you. Could we have your mailing address?   Thanks Miss Gall

This letter ended the correspondence for the summer, and when school began they each had a new penpal.

Dear Sarah.

You are right I am going to be out of school in one day. I will write to you in the summer. next year if you are not busy I will write to you. Because Iamin miss galls class in grade 3.Thank you for being my penpal.Have a good summer write back soon before its to late Your pal Greg.

~~(~): Greg ~~ublic School

Thursday, June 23, 1998 9:32:47 AM
Message

From: Molly F. Gall
Subject: Re(2): Greg
To: [Sarah]

Cc:

Thursday June 23, 1998

Dear Sarah,

You are right. I am going to be out of school in one day. I will write to you in the summer. Next year if you are not busy, I will write to you, because I am in Miss Gall's class in Grade 3. Thank you for being my penpal. Have a good summer. Write back soon before it's too late.

Your pal, Greg

Overall, their letters have a strong vitality. The electronic aspect of communication has not dulled the human interaction and obvious caring for each other. It is impossible to know if this same degree of attachment would have developed if Greg and Sarah had not been paired in the penpal program first.

A CASE STUDY: MATT AND RON

In this case, Matt, the student, began an e-mail correspondence with a complete stranger (who was actually the teacher's brother-in-law). Matt, a more able grade two student, had a keen interest in computers and spent a lot of time sending e-mail and surfing the net on his home computer. Matt was also an avid reader with above average ability.

Matt and Ron both had a very keen and highly developed interest in, and knowledge of, baseball. Ron was quite impressed that a grade two student knew so much about the game. He lent one of his most prized baseball books, a baseball dictionary, to Matt. Matt was thrilled by the gesture, and he carried the book with him wherever he went. When it was time to return the book, his teacher suggested that Matt might want to send Ron an e-mail to thank him.

Matt was an independent writer. He worked in Clarisworks for his draft, which was printed and edited with him. The letter was typed online and sent as an e-mail.

Tuesday May, 26 1998

Dear Ron, I am a student in miss Gall's class. She told me that you are a real baseball fan like me. She also told me that you like the montreal expos. I lik~~e the expos and the~~ Tronto blue jays. I wanted to see if y~~ ~~ I want to give you a quiz. Hears the
Here's

Do you know who holds the amera~~ ~~

Do you know who leads the blue ja~~ ~~

Do you Know who holds the nash~~ ~~
National

Do you know a lot about comput~~ ~~

This is a baseball joke do you kn~~ ~~ the outfiled?
outfield?

Thank you for loaning me the b~~ ~~
Matt

-----Original Message-----
From: Molly F. Gall
To:
Date: May 28, 1998 4:35 PM
Subject: baseball

>Tuesday, May 26, 1998
>
>
>Dear Ron,
>
>I am a student in Miss Gall's class. She told me that you are a real baseball fan like me. She also told me that you like the Montreal Expos. I like the Expos, and Toronto Blue Jays. I wanted to see if you know what I do, so I want to give you a quiz. Here's the quiz.
>
>Do you know who holds the American lead in homers?
>
>Do you know who leads the Blue Jays in home runs?
>
>Do you know who holds the National lead in homers?
>
>Do you know a lot about computers?
>
>This is a baseball joke. Do you know why a frog is good for the outfield?
>
>Thankyou for loaning me the baseball dictionary.
>Bye, from Matt
>
>
>
>

Printed by: Public S~~ ~~
Title: Re: baseball

         Thursday, May 28, 1998~~ ~~
         Message

From: Ron
Subject: Re: baseball
To: Molly F. Gall
Attachments: Internet He~~ ~~

hey matt! how are you doing?

thanks for the e-mail, and you're we~~lcome~~
on of those books you can pick up, open up anywhere and sta~~rt~~
enjoy!

quiz answers: (let me know how i did?)

american league home run leader? (as of pre games thursday may 28) alex rodriguez of the mariners with 19. "jr" is right behind with 18.

jose canseco leads the jays with 17.

in the 'senior circuit' it's mark mcgwire of the cards way out in front (of andres galarraga) with 25 dingers. (do you think he'll match 61??)

not as much as i'd like to.

because he can catch flies.

now matt: a question for you! in baseball terms what's a "can of corn"?
I think you know where to find the answer to that one!

listen to miss gall. she's a smart person and can teach you mauch.

have a great weekend!

regards,

Ron's reply was a variation of the standard friendly letter format. It also contained several grammatical errors, for like many adult e-mail users, he prefers to type e-mail without using upper case letters. Thus, Ron's letters might be considered a vernacular e-mail.

Ron and Matt are soul mates — both are consumed by baseball and thoroughly enjoy talking to someone who shares their passion. Matt makes this evident in his very first letter, by establishing a "baseball trivia" format. Ron picks up on this, adding the present baseball season to the trivia questions in his reply. Matt and Ron combine baseball shorthand and everyday vocabulary. More striking, is that they use language in deeply meaningful ways to both of them. Through this use of language, they establish a strong human relationship.

E-mail afforded both Matt and Ron the opportunity to respond to each other's e-mails quickly. Matt started his reply the day Ron's letter was downloaded. E-mail was an extracurricular activity, so Matt took a couple of days to reply. On his second day of writing, he recruited help from his classmate Chris. Matt remembered to put the greeting on a separate line. Most of his sentences started with a capital and had appropriate end punctuation. Matt's revisions were not made on his draft but on the final copy for Ron. Ron, like Matt, was quick to reply. Ron's letter again demonstrates the e-mail vernacular noted above, but this does not detract from the flow of the e-mail or from the relationship that is developing between these two.

Friday May,29 1998

Dear ron
I gess those were to easy for you, They were right. Whats a can of corn thats an easy one it is an easily caght fly ball. What kind of muisc do you like? and when was the first all star game.And if you do were was it played?

Tuesday, June 2 1998
I'm sorry about the dlay I never get my letters done by the weekend. Miss Gall knows that anwser. The expos play on saterday on TSN at seven.
were did you get the baseball dictionary? because I want it! i whine about it all day because I want it. when was exhibition stadium first bult? What do robbers do when they play baseball? This is my friend chris. He likes baseball but I like it better. this is chris hi ron me and Matt like your baseball dictionary. Do you like your baseball dictionary? How does a baseball player hold his bat? heres another joke for you how do players keep cool?

see you ron from matt

P.S. and chris

uesday, June 02, 1998 3:12:06 PM
Page 1 of 1

Friday May 29, 1998

Dear Ron,

I guess those questions were too easy for you. They were right. What's a can of corn? That's an easy one. It is an easily caught fly ball. What kind of music do you like? When was the first all star game played. Where was it played? Miss Gall knows that answer. The Expos play on Saturday on TSN at seven.

Tuesday, June 2, 1998

I'm sorry about the day. I never get my letters done in one day. Where did you get the baseball dictionary? Because I want it. I whine about it all day because I want one. When was Exhibition stadium first built? What do robbers do when they play baseball? This is from my friend Chris. He likes baseball, but I like it more. Do you like your baseball dictionary> How does a baseball player hold his bat? Here's another hoke for you, How do players keep cool?
See you Ron, from Matt
P.S. and from Chris (who helped)

Tuesday, June 02, 1998 10:17:29 AM
Message

From: Ron
Subject: Re: baseball
To: Molly F. Gall   1K
Attachments: Internet Header

hey matt:

baseball first all star game was played at chicagos' comiskey park in 1933. at american league won 4-2. (miss gall knew that!?? wow - i told you she was smart!)

other answers: rock, jazz, country, classical, and blues.

the baseball dictionary was a gift from my wife. i don't know where she bought it; however, you could take note of the author and the publishing company and order it through a book store.

you got me on when exhibition stadium was built. when?

robbers 'steal'. players keep cool by 'fanning'??   and how do ball players hold a bat?

thanks for the expos game reminder for saturday. i'll be watching!

take good care of my book, and write back when you get a chance.

regards,

ron

p.s. hi chris.

In his next e-mail to Ron, Matt started experimenting with different fonts.

Matt finishes this letter by mentioning his interest in country and classical music (he had been told that Ron was a DJ for the local country radio station).

Firday. June. 5th 1998
Hi Ron
How are you doing? the exibition stadium was built 1977. Ball platers hold a bat by is wings. you got the rest of the awnsers right. You are right Miss Gall is smart. Did you now that the Montreal Expos are secn last in the nashionl leahg. The Tronoto Blue Jays are thred in the leahg. I love contruy music and like some classical. bye bye Ron!!!!!

Matt and Ron continue the question–answer format. Matt follows the pattern Ron establishes of talking about both baseball history and the present season.

Ron's next e-mail to Matt had to be re-typed because there was a lot of computer text code mixed in the text, making it very difficult to read.

Ron's e-mail contained a lot of computer code and had to be retyped for clarity. This is one of the kinds of glitches that can occur in e-mail exchanges and it can be time consuming.

Printed by: · Public School
Title: more baseball

Sunday, June 14, 1998 2:46:34 PM
Message

From: Ron
Subject: more baseball
To: Molly F. Gall   1K
Attachments: Internet Header

```
<!DOCTYPE HTML PUBLIC "-//        W3 HTML//EN">
<HTML>
<HEAD>

<META content=text/html;char
<META content="'MSHTML 4.
</HEAD>
<BODY>
<DIV>hey matt: </DIV>
<DIV> </DIV>
<DIV>the first year the jays
however; it was built <EM>lo
<DIV>yes, i know the expos
dollars and having to unloa
(shrug)</DIV>
<DIV>what do you think of
amazing?  and on top of that, he
gentle man!  this would be the year for him (<EM>or so
62 homes runs, what with the expansion clubs, and the deluting of
pitching.  what do you think?  will he (or someone else) finally break
```

Sunday, June 14, 1998

Hey Matt;

The first year the Jays played at Exhibition stadium was 1977, however it was built before that. Yes, I know the Expos are struggling this year, chalk it up to dollars and having to unload all their best players again! What do yoiu think of Mark Mcgwire's home run prowess? Isn't he amazing? On top of that, he's not a jerk but a polite, and gentle man! This would be the year for him to hit 62 home runs, what, with the expansion clubs, and the deluting of pitching. What do you think? Will he finally break the record? Enjoy your last couple of weeks at school Matt! and be nice to Miss Gall.

Regards, Ron

Tuesday, June 16, 1998

Hey Ron

Thanks for telling me about the blue jays stadium I had it mixed up. Any ways about mark he does have some amazing home run powerss. But the ameracan players are geting good start like players in the other legk. I do think that mark will beat the record. Did you know that jose cansaco just came out of a two week slunp and the last five games he has got 10 hits and he has got 19 steals. The blue jays have never had a 30-30 man can you beleve it. Have the Montrueal Expos haver had a 30-30 man?

got to go regards, Matt

---

about the Blue Jays he does have some amazing home run prowess. But the American players are getting good starting players from the other league. I do think that Mark will beat the record. Did you know that Jose Cansaco just came out of a two week slump and the last five games he has got 10 hits and he has got 19 steals? The Blue Jays have never has a 30-30 man, can you believe it? Have the Montreal Expos ever had a 30-30 man? Miss Gall says that you are going to see an Expos game this weekend. Have fun!! My Mom says that I can keep writing to you this summer because I have an email address at home. I will give it to you next time I write.

got to go regards, Matt

Matt appropriates some of Ron's vocabulary in his response (home run "prowess"; "regards"). In the following letter, Ron continues to use both baseball-specific media vocabulary and words well beyond most grade two children, such as "prolific." However, he seems to realize that this is fine for Matt, who, with his gifts in language and his passion for baseball, responds well to this enrichment. This e-mail correspondence continued over the summer, and on into the next school year.

Printed by: Public School   Tuesday, June 23, 1998 10:57:01 AM
Title: Re: more baseball   Page 1 of 2

Tuesday, June 16, 1998 1:01:39 PM
Message

From: Ron
Subject: Re: more baseball
To: Molly F. Gall   1K
Attachments: Internet Header

hey matt! i don't belive the expos have even had a 30–30 man. andre dawson clubbed 32 home runs in 1983, in '82 he swiped 39 bases. so close eh? the most prolific base stealer was ron leflore who stole 97 in 1980. as a matter of fact i watch him steal #96, and #97 that year. it was in montreal at the end of the season (against the phillies, i think). re: mark mcgwire. i think if anybody is going to break the record this will be the year, and it sure appears mr. mcgwire has the skill to do it, but so to others - canseco, griffey, rodrequez, etc. it will make the stretch run interesting to say the least. and yes, i'm off to montreal saturday for the expos/braves game, then hit ottawa on sunday for the triple a lynx/durham bulls match. enjoy your last days at school! say hi to miss gall for me! mt home e-mail address ls

regards, ron

Over time, Matt and Ron exchanged thoughts about other aspects of their lives besides baseball; but, always, their shared passion for baseball and for talking about baseball is what kept their relationship strong and full of energy.

Keypal Pilot

The following year, Greg and Matt's teacher changed from a combined grade one and two class to a grade three class. Many of the same children from the previous year were in her class again. This provided an opportunity to have some students communicate with their penpals via e-mail, comparing their experiences to those of students who were communicating with regular penpal letters.

Since there were four computer stations in the classroom, it was logical to choose four children in this pilot project. The children who were chosen had to have a fair degree of competence and confidence with computers, and they had to prefer to write to their penpals in this fashion. Similarly, older penpals who were interested in corresponding by e-mail were matched.

The deadlines and basic structure were the same for keypals as they were for penpals. The keypals therefore used the format of a friendly letter with date, greeting, and closing. Like the penpals, they were to ask at least three questions and to give news or information to their keypals.

At the beginning, the four young keypals were very excited to be involved with this new endeavor. For their first letter they each had a printout of their keypal's e-mail in front of them to work from, parallel to the way things operated for the penpals. Their rough draft letters were done in Clarisworks and were printed out and edited with assistance. Each child then keyed in a final copy that the teacher sent through her e-mail.

As the year progressed, there appeared to be a decline in the enthusiasm of the young keypals. They were disappointed by the fact that their classroom penpal counterparts were receiving their letters in brightly decorated envelopes. The letters themselves often included colorful decorations and illustrations. These features were lacking in the e-mail letters that the keypals received.

Over the year, the teacher tried to add graphics for the e-mail children. You need to know how to do it, or have time to learn, or the results can be less successful than the children desire. The keypals were only able to include rough illustrations that they managed to create with the Clarisworks program or sometimes by using keyboard symbols to create a larger illustration. Yet, for children of this age, these illustrations were not nearly as captivating as the brightness and allure of the penpal letters with their special stationery, incorporation of contemporary animation figures, and even photographs. Some of the keypals tried to compensate for this by sending jokes back and forth much as Ron and Matt had done in their e-mail communication.

The young keypals also sometimes became frustrated with the computer technology, such as when the computer did not save their letters properly, and they had to re-write much or all of them; when they were ready but unable to write their letters because the computers were "down"; when the printer was not working and they could not print out the letters; and when the teacher could not get online. Young children have limited patience when it comes to problems such as these: They want things to happen immediately. Their frustration was understandable, but the solutions to many of the problems were often beyond a teacher's control.

When the keypal program ended in March (the same time as penpals), the three remaining keypals (one had moved) all agreed that if given the choice, the next time they would rather be in the penpal program. This was a limited pilot. Only a few of the children in the class were involved. Greater satisfaction might have been achieved with slightly older children, or by having the whole class correspond by e-mail.

Given this pilot experience, we outline some conditions that we feel are essential for a successful keypal program.

Setting up a Keypal Program

In setting up a class-wide keypal program, the following items are necessary.

Recommendations for a Keypal Program

1. **Availability of a sufficient number of computers with Internet access and a printer.**
   The printer is an essential part of the keypal program — without one, it is very difficult to keep copies of first drafts, which are key items for assessment. Without the printer, it is much more difficult for the children to work from their keypal's letter.

   A color printer with sufficient budget to supply ink for a full classroom of letter writers is the ideal. A color printer helps to make the letters more appealing, especially if attachments are used instead of sending the whole correspondence merely in e-mail.

2. **A teacher with a strong computer knowledge of e-mail, word processing programs, computer graphics, and sending and receiving attachments.**
   In the pilot, if a computer specialist had been available to help send and receive attachments, the letters could have been written on computer-generated stationery, and graphics could have been included in the text or at the bottom or top of a page.

3. **Students need to have basic computer comfort (basic keyboarding skills and knowledge of basic word processing programs such as Clarisworks, WordPerfect, Word).**
   These kinds of word processing programs are *very* important because they are more sophisticated than most word processing packages designed for young children. Keypals need software that allows them to import graphics, alter fonts, and write letters of whatever length they wish.

4. **A central e-mail account/address controlled by the classroom teacher.**
   The teacher needs to have control over access unless there is school board policy and parental permission for children to have their own accounts. (In the case studies of keypals above, older keypals wrote to their younger counterparts through the teacher's school e-mail address.)

5. **Keypals with e-mail addresses and consistent computer access.**
   Be sure that the other keypals can access their e-mail easily and consistently. If, for instance, your class is communicating with another class, that teacher must have the same amount of Internet access as you do, whether that means in their own room or in a school computer lab.

6. **Knowledge and consent of your principal and parents/guardians.**
   Given the vastness and the potential for misuse of the Internet, it is essential that the principal and parents/ guardians give permission for the children to engage in online correspondence. Close teacher supervision is crucial to ensure that children are safe in this correspondence.

7. **Mutually agreed upon deadlines for letters from both correspondents.**

The same kind of structure needs to exist in this regard for keypal correspondence as it does for penpal correspondence. Without deadlines, a teacher can find it difficult to maintain the organizational particulars needed to ensure that writing process sequences of editing and re-writing occur.

In addition, some people feel compelled to respond to e-mail immediately, and this kind of urgency is not what we promote. Rather, we wish correspondents to write thoughtfully and insightfully. In order to do so, they must be able to plan ahead, so they can put aside the necessary time to write an engaging letter.

8. **Mutually agreed upon structure and content of keypal/ e-mail letters (i.e., friendly letter format; use conventional spelling, grammar, and punctuation; ask each other questions; answer each other's questions; offer some new information).**

Although friends often use e-mail shorthand, such as eliminating upper case letters from their writing, part of the purpose of this correspondence is the development of fluency and control over standard writing conventions. Most children need to have models of standard conventions which they can use to support their own learning.

We have shown you in previous chapters just how strongly some children rely on their older correspondents' letters in writing their own letters. When older correspondents realize the degree to which their errors as well as their correctly used conventions are mirrored by the child's writing, there is usually no problem in compliance with this.

Keypal Web Sites

Some teachers may wish to find other classes at the same age level with which to establish a keypal program. The Appendix includes an annotated list of web sites as a starting point. Although we have explored these web sites, we cannot speak to their integrity other than the information that we give. In addition, many sites and addresses change or disappear completely after a while. As with most things on the Internet, teachers need to take a "buyer beware" approach to this information.

If you wish to investigate the integrity of a site, ask the site operators to send addresses of other teachers who have used the site. Other teachers may well provide the strongest reference check. Ask pertinent questions related to things such as how long they have been involved with the site, the name and e-mail address of the teacher with whom they are corresponding, and the kinds of problems that they have encountered in the program. Then it is good to contact the second teacher to ensure the reliability of the information from the first teacher. This provides a double-check.

There are wonderful human connections to be made through use of the Internet. By exercising caution and notifying parents and principal of your intentions, most teachers will find an exciting link for their students.

Some Concluding Thoughts On Keypals

Given the successes as well as the challenges of the pilot keypal program with four children, there are certain cautionary statements we would like to make about keypal programs.

- *Children with basic language fluency*

The children who were keypals were selected first for having a basic language fluency and for their interest in participating in a keypal program. These children all knew letter formation, word boundary, and they had fluent spelling and decoding skills. Sufficient language fluency lets keypal children focus on meaning-making both in reading and writing their penpal letter rather than on word decoding or formation. They were able to generate ideas on their own in extending the conversation. The keypal children did not need the kind of assistance that emergent and early readers do in reading their keypals' letters or in responding to them.

- *Children with computer comfort*

Participation in the pilot was voluntary: Children had the option of using the computer and e-mail or of hand-writing their letters. As well as children's desire, the classroom teacher's judgment was essential in indicating whether or not children's skills were sufficient to enable them to work largely independently.

Even with only four children, computer glitches presented some time-consuming problems, including computer codes embedded in text and attachments that could not be downloaded or opened. Glitches are inevitable in technology, and the children need to be sufficiently independent in enough areas that computer difficulties do not present what is felt to be more than a mild annoyance. We think that trying to do a keypal program with children with fewer language or computer skills would become overwhelming for the classroom teacher.

- *The whole class is involved in the same type of program: keypal or penpal*

It is very difficult to operate both a penpal and a keypal program in the same room, so we advise against it. You can avoid several problems (such as technology glitches; the need for letter formation lessons and for keyboarding lessons; one set of children receive decorated letters but the other set does not) if there is only type of program operating.

• *Letter deadline complexities*

E-mail is fast and very compelling. This is as true for children as it is for adults. The older keypals usually answered as soon as they got their e-mail. Their responses had to be held so that penpal students and keypal students would receive their letters and start their response letters at the same time. Any delays of this sort mean that letters can go astray before they reach their intended recipient. It can also be very difficult if the keypal students know a letter has arrived, but they cannot respond.

• *Consistency in the type of letters received*

Because most of the class was involved in a penpal program, most of the class received letters in creative and brightly colored envelopes that were compelling and inviting from the first time anyone saw them. The children in the keypal program missed the bright colors, whimsical decorations, and enclosures that are so much a part of the penpal letters in our program.

If your classroom does not have a color printer or if the older keypal does not have a computer program that creates color graphics, it is difficult to make keypal letters as visually appealing as the penpal letters.

• *Ability to help each other solve writing problems*

When children are working on the same kinds of writing, they have more opportunities to share knowledge and to learn from each other. The four pilot keypal children would often leave their computers and wander around to look at other children's letters. This is a good way to get ideas and to share knowledge. However, because they were working on computers, they often had problems that only someone else doing the task in the same way could help them solve.

Throughout this book we have stressed the community aspect of penpal letter writing. We are uncertain how the community aspect would play out if all children were keypals. We think that it is still possible and desirable to promote the activity as a community of writers; but, we know that different daily rituals would need to be developed. The computer is a very different writing tool than the pencil, and it engenders very different kinds of human interaction between students.

• *Compatible and reliable computer hardware and software*

It is vitally important to have reliable computers, programs, printers, and e-mail access because a keypal program depends on this technology. The computers and software must also be able to translate from one to the other if attachments and graphics are included. Even with good hardware and software, teachers will need a certain degree of flexibility, for system problems can occur when no one is able to get online. At these times, teachers will need to move into other activities with the ability to return to the computers when the system is back online. Thus, if a school computer lab is being used for a keypal program, the teacher must build in accommodations for the lab-booking system ahead of time.

With all these conditions in check, one should be able to set up and run a highly effective keypal program. The pilot keypal program demonstrated that the keypal environment is very different from the pencil and paper penpal environment. A keypal program offers different possibilities but also requires different skill levels in both language and computing.

10

Fostering a Community of Reader/Writers

In the opening chapter of this book, we talked about skill development through friendship and about going beyond rote skill development to using written language to support human connection and caring. We feel it is important to articulate the sociocultural theory that underpins the practices we advocate throughout the book.

Across the English-speaking world, teachers increasingly face issues involving accountability measures. Children of seven or eight years of age write provincial or national tests to measure their abilities in reading, writing, and mathematics. The practice is controversial; however, the reality is that such testing now exists in many jurisdictions and will remain a part of public education for a considerable time.

With the intensity of the testing and the public reporting of results of individual schools, teachers need to help their children do well on the tests. This carries both positive and negative ramifications, for along with what is often indisputable higher achievement when teachers "teach to the test," there can be a loss of learning experiences that teachers deeply value. Activities such as class trips, choral speaking, reading books for pleasure...and writing to penpals...may seem to be less directly related to test performance and, hence, give way to activities such as worksheets, which replicate the kinds of tasks found on the tests.

Revising teaching strategies to "teach to the test" to support high test scores is an understandable response. However, one reason for writing this book was to demonstrate just how something like a penpal program can contribute directly to children's literacy skill development — in very accountable ways. Assessment practices and the assessment exemplars in this book were carefully selected to help teachers understand how and why penpal writing can help children achieve curricular expectations.

In all communities, experts have a responsibility to help novices learn. This is no less true in the penpal community. It is crucially important that teachers recognize themselves as the expert writers in their classroom writing community. Part of the teacher's responsibility is always to help children become more fluent and skilled writers and readers. This involves helping children to build their skills and understanding, as well as celebrating what they have achieved. We also wish to encourage teachers to not lose sight of those deep reasons that brought many of us into teaching: a desire to help children learn to love language and feel the satisfaction that comes when one's work is acknowledged and celebrated. Nothing matches the light in a child's eyes when she or he receives a letter from a person who devotes time and caring to just them. Penpal writing provides a sense of well-being that is evident in the laughter and excitement of the experience. We must find ways to maintain these kinds of learning experiences alongside the new accountability.

Social and Cultural Theories of Learning: Communities of Practice

When a whole classroom is engaged in a penpal program in the ways that we have described, each child becomes a legitimate member of the reading/writing community — regardless of their skill level. Ongoing participation in any type of activity — scientific investigation, mathematical problem-solving, or lifelong reading and writing — depends as much on the individual's self-perception or feeling that she or he belongs as it does on their ability level.

Etienne Wenger explains that people form opinions about their own agency and their ability to carry through with their intentions based on the kinds of everyday social practices in which they participate. Other sociocultural theorists such as Dyson, Lave, Rogoff, Vygotsky, and Wertsch round out this concept, alerting us to look at the daily rituals enacted by children, to re-appraise the types of interactions we encourage and discourage in our classrooms, and to assess the degree of participation in, and mutual construction of, meaning to which our students have access because of our classroom organization.

The approach that we espouse throughout this book associates the reading and writing practices of the penpal program with a community of literacy practitioners. The children negotiate their penpal practices with each other, with the teacher, and with their penpals. They appropriate words and ideas, they resist some words and ideas that are given to them, and they introduce their own new topics and questions. They are mutually engaged in the practice of letter writing and reading, and regardless of their skill level, there are support practices in place that enable every child to participate.

We emphasize a collective practice in the ways we propose a penpal program should operate. It could be possible, for instance, to run a penpal program without any formal whole class sharing of letters. However, we strongly encourage whole class sharing, both in a formal practice of sharing letters and also informally as the children write their letters, talk to each other, look at each others' letters, and carry those ideas back to their own writing. Increasingly, researchers are identifying the amount of learning that occurs when classroom organization encourages these types of interactions.

From a sociocultural point of view, these practices underscore the collaborative nature of the penpal enterprise in that all children share the same repertoires of penpal writing and reading. The children increasingly share a history of engagement that generates a social energy around the letter writing and reading, which, in turn, encourages reluctant and less-skilled writers to participate. Teachers involved with this program continue to comment on that social energy as one of the most powerful features of the program.

Social and Cultural Theories of Learning: Identity

Many of us would quickly agree that the activities we take part in constitute the features of who we are: Our identities are formed both by self-perception and by the perceptions of others. In the penpal program, all children receive, read, and write penpal letters, allowing each child to form their own identity as writer and reader and be affirmed in this identity by classmates and older penpals.

Wenger talks about identity in practice. There are multiple ways in which identity is linked to practice, including the following:

- *Identity as negotiated experience*
  We define who we are by the ways we experience our selves through participation, as well as by the ways we and others reify our selves.

- *Identity as community membership*
  We define who we are by the familiar and the unfamiliar.

- *Identity as a relation between the local and the global*
  We define who we are by negotiating local ways of belonging to broader constellations and of manifesting broader styles and discourses. (1998:149)

A penpal program that follows the practices we have described supports literacy identity development as negotiation, as community membership, and as belonging both to the local classroom community of writers and to a more global community. The larger goals focus on having the children feel that part of who they are as persons includes reading and writing; that they read and write to build and maintain meaningful relationships with other people; and that the reading and writing bring them pleasure and satisfaction, even when they involve hard work.

Building a Community of Reader/Writers

The penpal program is not the only way to build a community of reader/writers, but it is one way. At the beginning, building a whole program can feel overwhelming, so it is important to keep the larger picture in mind. The particulars of practice build over time. And at first, the single most important thing is to support each child in her or his reading and writing, so that each one feels that they are legitimate members of this penpal community. Celebrate the letters that come and go; and, celebrate the children for their participation.

Appendix

Penpal Web Sites

1. KidsCom: Make New Friends
http://www.kidscom.com/orakc/
This web site promotes and encourages its users to sign up for a keypal through the Find a Key Pal program. The site includes a graffiti wall and a chat line for its users. The user cannot access the graffiti wall without a password and user ID. There are two possible graffiti walls for children to access, the Graffiti Wall Chat for children eleven years old and younger and the Teen Wall for children twelve years old and up. The chat lines are open from 3:00 p.m. to 10:00 p.m., seven days a week. The Key Pal program is set up in a formal and very detailed manner to protect its users. A permission form is also signed by the user when creating a keypal.

2. Epals.com
http://www.epals.com/index.htm.
This web site has existed since 1996, and it promotes the world's largest K–12 online classroom and electronic penpal network. Some special features include "Teacher Moderated Email," "International Weather," "Instant Language Translation to and from six different languages," and maps of the world. Teachers can register their classroom here to find an Epal classroom.

3. Pen-Pal Exchanges
Wysiwyg://340/http://www.eskimo.com/
This web site promotes numerous penpal exchanges, including a penpals program for gifted children. For the most part, it targets individual students rather than whole classrooms. The site gives a guide on how to apply to various penpal programs, but does not provide links to any of the other sites it promotes. It simply acts as an information guide.

4. The Kids on the Web: Pen Pals
http://www.zen.org/~brendan/kids-pen.htm
This web site is maintained by KIDLINK, which has aimed at getting 10–15-year-olds involved in global dialogue since 1990. It directs children and their parents to different penpal sites including specialized sites such as Girl Pals and SAPE (Soviet- American Penfriend Exchange). Links to these penpal sites are not accessible by this page.

5. AGW's Free Penpal Spectacular!
http://www.agirlsworld.com
This web site is directed at girls aged 7–17 and allows females to find penpals without publishing their e-mail addresses. Users can create an online profile and change it at any time.

6. Woody's Favorite Web Sites
http://www.esd.k12.ca.us
This web site lists Woody's favorite sites. Children can access different links such as a 4Kids Treehouse, Kid Pub, and an International Kids Space, which allows children the opportunity to form keypals with other children around the world.

7. Webcrawler People and Chat Channel
http://www.webcrawler.com/people_and_cha...ls/?
This web page allows and gives the user a list of penpal web sites. You can access different links from this page (such as the game and chat room). Under each web site certain criteria are listed. Some program sites match by age, sex, geographic location, interest, (dis)abilities, etc.

8. Links2Go: Pen Pals
http://www.links2go.com
This site gives the user potential web sites where penpal links may be established. You can type in a search title or go directly to each site.

9. Pen Pal Planet
http://home.epix.net/~ppplanet
This web site promotes international penpal programs with individuals from Russia and Europe. It is a free program and does not indicate or specify the age of the user. The home page has many different information options and also offers or gives the user a choice of e-mail penpals.

10. The DinPals Penpals Page
http://members.aol.com/kidz4peace/dinopals/penpal.htm
This web site advocates Penpal Friendliness for Peace and for letter writing penpals (rather than keypals). This site also gives the addresses and contacts for different organizations. The site does not allow the user to access any of the site lists. It is designed for children (one of its user aims is Boy Scout and Girl Scout troops, and other youth groups).

11. KIDSWORLD!!...by Kids & for Kids!
http://www.bconnex.net/~kidworld
This web site is geared towards children. Many activities are accessible on this web site, including monthly writing contests. Users can sign up for the keypals program, which requires leaving name, address, and other personal details.

Language Arts Web Sites

There is a remarkable amount of English language arts information available on the Internet. The following web site list highlights sites of particular interest to educators in Canada, the United States, and England. Educators will find these sites of value in relation to curriculum documents and expectations, provincial and national testing results, learning resources, and links to other educational sites.

Canada

www.edu.gov.on.ca

This is the site of the Ministry of Education of Ontario. Curriculum documents are available at this site, including learning expectations at each grade level. There are many links to other sites, including Canada's SchoolNet, the ERIC educational database, the U.S. Department of Education, and the U.K. Department for Education and Employment.

www.bced.gov.bc.ca

This is the site of the Ministry of Education of British Columbia. In addition to curriculum documents there are other teaching resources such as integrated resource packages (IRPs) and valuable links to other educational sites.

www.curriculum.org

This site belongs to the Ontario Curriculum Clearing House, an independent educational agency. The learning resources are especially valuable here, and there are educational links often not found elsewhere, such as TVOntario and the Asia Pacific Foundation.

www.schoolnet.ca

This is the site for SchoolNet, the Canadian site that serves to support Canadian content and resources in teaching. The site is valuable for both teachers and students, including learning resources, available government and non-government programs, and the Kidsworld pages, which sponsor contests and ways for students to get published.

United States

www.ed.gov

This is the site for the U.S. Department of Education. Reports from a wide array of national initiatives are available here, including things like results from the National Assessment of Educational Progress (the U.S. national report card), the America Reads Challenge, and national education statistics.

www.ncte.org

The National Council of Teachers of English site has information on its many conferences and publications, as well as learning resources, and valuable links to other English, language arts, reading, and writing sites.

www.reading.org

The International Reading Association web site has information about conferences and conventions, its multiple councils and affiliates, international projects, publications, and research.

England

www.nc.uk.net

This is the site for the National Curriculum for England with links to the sites for Northern Ireland, Scotland, and Wales. The complete National Curriculum 2000 is now available, as well as information about the various educational initiatives in place in the U.K. These initiatives include the National Literacy Strategy, the Year 7 Catch-up Programs, Beacon schools and Excellence in Cities. The site also includes an extraordinary number of links to other U.K. education sites and specific information and learning resources.

www.dfee.gov.uk

This site belongs to the Department for Education and Employment (DfEE) — or what is called the department/ministry of education in other countries. As well as its links to other government educational sites, it also carries statistics on performance tables available for primary and secondary schools, by local education authority (school board). The site is unique in the degree of its public availability of local performance on national testing.

www.qca.org.uk

The Qualifications and Curriculum Authority (QCA) is responsible for monitoring and reviewing the National Curriculum, including development and management of the national assessment system. The site contains standards reports, information about the national Literacy Hours, and the Framework for Teaching, with very specific guidelines for teachers and schools.

www.ngfl.gov.uk

The National Grid for Learning (NGfL) site has many resources for learning, including links to museums, libraries, and other actual learning resources. In addition, the international networks available through links are very impressive, including sites such as Canada's SchoolNet, the European SchoolNet, and the Commonwealth Institute.

www.ofsted,gov.uk

The Office for Standards in Education (OfSTED) is independent from the governmental Department for Education and Employment and is responsible for inspection of British schools. This site enables public access to reports of inspections of individual schools, across the country.

References and Suggested Reading

Ahlberg, J. & A. (!986). *The Jolly Postman, or Other People's Letters*. Little, Brown & Co.

Bahktin, M.M. (1981). (Ed., M. Holquist). The dialogic imagination. Austin, TX. University of Austin Press.

Barr, R., M.L. Kamil, P. Mosenthal, & P.D. Pearson (Eds.) (1991). *Handbook of reading research*, Vol. II. New York: Longman.

Bereiter, C. & Scardamalia, M. (1987). *The psychology of written composition*. Hillsdale, NJ: Lawrence Erlbaum Associates.

Berrill, D.P. & Gall, M. (1999). On the carpet: Emergent writer/readers' letter sharing in a penpal program. *Language Arts*, 76 (6), 470-478.

Calkins, L. M. (1986). *The art of teaching writing*. Portsmouth, NH: Heinemann Educational Books.

Clay, Marie. (1975). *What did I write?* Exeter, NH: Heinemann Educational Books.

Dyson, A.H. (1989). *Multiple worlds of child writers: Friends learning to write*. New York: Teachers College Press.

Dyson, A.H. (1995). Weaving possibilities: Rethinking metaphors for early literacy development. *Reading Teacher*, 44 (3), 202-213.

Farr, Marcia. (Ed.) (1985). *Advances in writing research, Vol. I: Children's early writing development*. Norwood, NJ: Albex.

Flower, L. (1988). *Problem solving strategies for writing*. New York: Harcourt.

Gentry, J.R. (1987) *Spel ... Is A Four-letter Word*. Richmond Hill, Canada: Scholastic.

Graves, D. (1994). *A fresh look at writing*. Portsmouth, NH: Heinemann.

Irwin, J.W. & Doyle, M.A. (Eds.) (1992). *Reading/writing connections: Learning from research*. Newark, DE: International Reading Association.

Lave, J & Wenger, E. (1991). *Situated learning: Legitimate peripheral participation*. Cambridge, UK: Cambridge University Press.

Mason, J. (Ed.) (1989) *Reading and writing connections*. Needham Heights, MA: Allyn & Bacon.

McGinley, W & Kamberelis, G. (1996). Maniac Magee and Ragtime Tumpie: Children negotiating self and world through reading and writing. *Research in the Teaching of English*, 30 (10, 75–113).

Ministry of Education and Training of Ontario. (1999). *The Ontario Curriculum B Exemplars Grades 1–8: Writing*. Toronto: Ontario Ministry of Education and Training.

Myers, M. & Spalding, E. (Eds.). (1997). *Assessing Student Performance Grades K–5* (Standards Exemplar Series). Urbana, IL: National Council of Teachers of English.

Newkirk, T. (1989) *More Than Stories: The Range of Children's Writing*. Portsmouth, NH: Heinemann Educational Books.

Newkirk, T. & Atwell, N. (Eds.) (1982) *Understanding Writing: Ways of Observing, Learning and Teaching*. Chelmsford, MA: The Northeast Regional Exchange, Inc.

Qualifications and Curriculum Authority (2000). *The National Curriculum for England 2000*. London. Her Majesty's Stationary Office (HMSO),

Rankin, J.L. (1992). Connecting literacy learners: A pen pal project. *The Reading Teacher*, 46 (3):204-214.

Rogoff. B. (1990). *Apprenticeship in thinking: Cognitive development in social context*. New York: Oxford University Press.

Rosen, B.(1988). *And none of it was nonsense: The power of storytelling in school*. London: Mary Glasgow Publications Ltd.

Sperling, M. (1996). Revisiting the writing-speaking connection: Challenges for research on writing and writing instruction. *Review of Educational Research*, 66 (1), 53–86.

Standards for the Assessment of Reading and Writing. (1994). International Reading Association and the National Council of Teachers of English. USA.

Standards for the English Language Arts. (1996). International Reading Association and the National Council of Teachers of English. USA.

Sulzby, Elizabeth (1992) Research directions: Transitions from emergent to conventional writing. *Language Arts*, 69:290–297.

Tarasoff, Mary (1990). *Spelling: Strategies you can teach*. Victoria, B.C.: Active Learning Institute.

Teale, W.H. & Suzby, E. (Eds.) (1986). *Emergent literacy: Writing and reading*. Norwood, NJ: Ablex.

Vygotsky, L.S. (1978). *Mind in society: The development of higher psychological processes*. Cambridge, MA: Harvard University Press.

Wells, G. & Chang-Wells, G.L. (1992). *Constructing knowledge together: Classrooms as centers of inquiry and literacy*. Portsmouth, NH: Heinemann.

Wenger, E. (1998). *Communities of practice: Learning, meaning, and identity*. Cambridge, UK: Cambridge University Press.

Wertsch, J. (1991). *Voices of the mind: A sociocultural approach to mediated action*. Cambridge, MA: Harvard University Press.

Western Canadian Protocol for Collaboration in Basic Education. (1996). The Western Canadian Common Curriculum Framework for English Language Arts K–12. The Governments of Alberta, British Columbia, Manitoba, Northwest Territories, Saskatchewan & Yukon Territory.

Index